# Spaghetti From The Chandelier

# Spaghetti From The Chandelier
### ...AND OTHER HUMOROUS ADVENTURES OF A MINISTER'S FAMILY

## RUTH TRUMAN

Illustrated by Tim Truman

Abingdon Press
Nashville

Spaghetti from the Chandelier
. . . and Other Humorous Adventures of a Minister's Family

*Copyright © 1984 by Abingdon Press*

**Library of Congress Cataloging in Publication Data**

TRUMAN, RUTH, 1931–
  Spaghetti from the chandelier.
  1. Truman, Ruth, 1931–      2. Truman, Lee. 3. Clergymen's
wives—United States—Biography. 4. Methodist Church—United
States—Clergy—Biography. 5. United Methodist Church (U.S.)—
Clergy—Biography. I. Title.
BX8495.T79A37      1984      287'.6'0924 [B]      83–14971

**ISBN 0-687-39146-6**

MANUFACTURED BY THE PARTHENON PRESS
NASHVILLE, TENNESSEE, UNITED STATES OF AMERICA

This book is dedicated to
the six people who made it possible:

LEE,
MARK, BECKY, TIM, NATHAN,

and ME . . .

and to all the people who fill its pages
and the pages of our lives.

# Contents

# Spaghetti From The Chandelier

# The Beginning

We were *so* young!

1

"The Methodist church is around the corner."

Blushing, my husband and I backed down the steps of the Roman Catholic church in the quiet New Jersey town. We had just arrived from California, and what did we know about churches anyway? Lee had never led a Methodist congregation in worship, and I had been taught to follow dutifully where he led me. . . .

Ducking as quickly as possible into our turquoise Plymouth coupe, we drove two-and-a-half blocks around the corner and down the main street. The church that awaited us there was not nearly so good-looking. It hadn't been painted for a long time. A few cars were parked along the adjacent curbs, but it was easy to tell that the church was not full to the doors! We parked in front of a house we guessed must be the parsonage (it was next to the church and far away from the neighbors) and headed for the tall double doors of the sanctuary.

We knew we couldn't just sneak in. This was obviously a town where everybody knew everybody. (Probably a courier had already brought the news that we had bungled into the Roman Catholic church.) Still, we weren't quite prepared to be met on the church steps by a woman carrying Communion trays—and wanting to know if "we're going to have Communion this morning?" Obviously she was ready to see that "we" did.

Communion. I could see the confusion play across Lee's face. He had never even been in a Methodist Communion service, let alone served one. "Why—I don't think we will. It's my first Sunday, and I think we'd better just get to know one another. . . ." His voice trailed away as the woman turned back abruptly in the direction from which she had come. Later we would discover that she lived across the street and kept careful watch over the church and the house—whether anyone wanted her to or not!

So what's so bad about not serving Communion on your first Sunday in a new parish? Nothing—unless it just happens to be Worldwide Communion Sunday! Probably not another church in Christendom passed up the event. . . . Perhaps we should have stopped right there. But thank goodness we didn't! So many more things were to happen that left us either gasping in embarrassment, laughing hysterically, or weeping until our tears were literally washed away. It would have been a shame to have missed it all!

This is the story of two people with a dream. It started in 1953 on the porch steps of the Roman Catholic church, and it continues today in California.

We share it with you in the hope that, if you are a layperson, you will receive new understanding and offer more forgiveness to your pastor; and if you are clergy you will take heart that you too will live through your immediate crisis . . . and maybe even the one that is coming tomorrow.

And someday you can tell *your* story. It will probably be just as wild!

## 2

We were *so* young! I was not quite twenty-two. Lee was twenty-four. And he had just been assigned to his first church.

But let me go back before the beginning. It really all started on the edge of a Georgia turnip field.

I had the audacity to fail the rabbit test the summer before—I was pregnant. Back in the aeons of history, circa 1952, no woman could teach in the state of Georgia after the third month of pregnancy, on the theory that it would warp the children if they saw a slightly warped figure. (I guess their mothers never got out of shape when they carried babies!) Consequently, the same day I failed the rabbit test in California I had to turn down a teaching contract in Georgia. That meant we would be going to seminary in Atlanta without an income.

With a loan from Lee's parents we had managed to buy a car—that turquoise coupe—and had put all our unearthly goods in it for the trek from California. Lee was a native Californian who would later tell people in New Jersey that if they thought their chances for heaven weren't too good, they should be sure to see California before they died. (We had guests for years when we finally settled there . . .)

But the point is that with no income except my substitute teaching, we arrived in Georgia late that summer unable to afford a regular place to live. So we scraped together $100 and bought a World War II-surplus army-green trailer and attempted to move it to the edge of the aforesaid turnip field. Of course the frame came out from under it when Lee hitched it to the car and tried to pull it. But a little welding took care of that. Later we would fix the caved-in roof, build in a bed, and paint it, making it into a lovely eighteen-foot home . . . except when it rained and the field turned to mud so deep we had to walk planks to get to the door.

But never mind all that. We were young and in love! It was our first home. Our first child was born while we lived there (and our bathroom was inside the landlady's house). And there were dogwood blossoms all around us in the springtime.

There were also ice ponds on the floor of the trailer in the winter. The drain pipe to the old-fashioned ice box would freeze solid in cold weather and the melting ice in the box dumped water onto the floor. The one-sheet washer was fine in the spring after Mark was born, but the next winter would be another matter. So the call from New Jersey that summer, at the end of Lee's first year of seminary, with the promise of a church and a house, was most welcome. There were seminaries in New Jersey as well as in Georgia.

What you don't know almost always saves you! A year by the

15

turnip field had not removed our idiotic, lovely naiveté. We were not even phased when the district superintendent casually mentioned that the church was available long past appointment time because the congregation had asked the former minister to move and then had refused to accept the assigned pastor—had even threatened to nail shut the doors of the church if he were sent there. For all we knew, this was normal. We were also sure that we would be loved by one and all. As it turned out, sometimes it was one, and sometimes it was all!

So that's how we happened to arrive in New Jersey that fateful Sunday morning. Our car was loaded with most of what we owned, and after the service was over (thank goodness!) we were shown around the parsonage—sure enough, it was the house we had parked in front of.

What a house! It was a century and a half old. For one hundred years it had been the church, then it had been moved down the hill to its new foundation, divided into two stories, and voila—a parsonage. Talk about vibes! There were some nights when I would believe the old church organ was still moaning and groaning through the walls.

Our walk through the house was revealing. The living room and study weren't bad, especially after a trailer by a turnip field. The center attraction of the dining room was a frazzled hole in the rug and the frame of the basement door didn't meet the wall—but I reasoned that my parts might not hang together too well either, by the time I was that old. Then we came to the kitchen. Sunny and bright, lots of cupboards, and barely attached linoleum-covered wallboard blowing gently in the September breeze. You could see through to the outside in several places.

Upstairs were two bedrooms, plus a room big enough to hold a sewing machine—if you had one. And a bathroom. This, we were soon to discover, was the most important room in the house. Since the church didn't have indoor facilities, the older women were accustomed to using the parsonage bathroom, rather than the outhouses, which stood prominently behind the church building.

That was the second thing I learned. The first was that I was going to live in this lovely old house *by myself* from 5:00 A.M. Tuesday until 5:00 P.M. Friday, while Lee was at school a hundred miles away. There was no police force in town, and a grove of huge trees stood between the parsonage and our nearest neighbor. The bedrooms were on the second story, and the only telephone was downstairs. To top it all off, the house was heated with a coal furnace, and I'd never built a coal fire in my life.

By Monday night, we were moved in—Lee, baby Mark, and I. Tuesday morning, right on schedule, Lee left for seminary. That night I moved the baby's bed into my bedroom, locked the house, locked the bedroom door (just *great* in case of fire!), went to bed, and stayed awake all night listening to the house. I would do that for a long time. . . .

Lee is not your typical person. That's why I married him. He stands out in a crowd. The first time I saw him, he was wearing jeans, engineer's boots, and an old camel's hair coat that he had slept in—after hitchhiking to Indiana from California. As I was soon to find out, he was not going to be very typical as a minister either. No Wednesday-night-Bible-study Sunday-morning-sermon minister this one!

He arrived home on schedule that Friday—and almost every Friday for two years—with his head full of ideas. First he must paint the church. It looked dreadful. And the house. He could get the fire company's ladder to reach the steeple. And the roof would need doing, too—there was no oil in the shingles. Of course, the outside of the building should be lighted so that people coming down Main Street would notice it. And the bell should ring—perhaps a carillon system in the steeple to play to the countryside. That was just the first Friday. . . .

Sunday number two came. Lee was in the bathroom shaving when the first knock came at the front door. Two of the ladies had come early to prepare their classroom, and could they please use the bathroom? Innocence to the rescue! The words "my husband is shaving" brought the strangest look to their faces. It never occurred to me to invite them in to wait. I was surprised that they had come for that purpose, since there were perfectly obvious outhouses behind the church.

Not long afterward, Lee proposed that the basement of the church be remodeled with wood paneling so there would be a pleasant hall for dinners and other meetings. Immediately, the ladies' class voted to underwrite the cost of two indoor restrooms, on the condition that they were soundproof (this was the reason the ladies preferred to use the parsonage bathroom) and that the outhouses were left standing, just in case the plumbing should ever fail!

Only years later did I discover that the restrooms were included because I had turned them away from the parsonage bathroom. The former minister's wife—with five small children—never had. Innocence had saved the day!

3

The second Sunday revealed another fact: we had a second church. It was a picturesque white country church, hovering protectively against the community cemetery. On a good Sunday, thirty people might be waiting for Lee to fly in: By the third year, he was arriving by yellow convertible and to save time, often left his pulpit robe on. It billowed around him just as if he actually were in an open cockpit.

A few Sundays were all we needed to get the art form correct. Lee would shake hands with the last parishioner in the town church, dash to his waiting car behind the parsonage, usually check to see if his wife and small son were in place, and tear out lickety-split on the twelve-minute drive to the country church.

Meanwhile, eight miles away, two boys were posted as sentinels. When they caught sight of our car coming down the road, robe flying and dust swirling, they gave the signal for the choir to start down the aisle. We would squeal to a stop just in time for Lee to step out of the car and into line behind the last choir member. Shaking the dust off your feet when you left a town had a literal meaning for us.

For you to fully understand the town church and the country church, you should know that each thought the other didn't belong on their pastoral circuit. And neither acknowledged the third church listed on the appointment, since it kept its doors closed rather than admit the black members of its community. We never did get that church open. . . .

The town church owned the parsonage, so it had first claim to the pastor, according to the members. The country church laughed about being the country cousin who kept the town church humble! But sometimes the joking got us into big trouble.

The weather was beginning to change, and Lee was having no luck with the furnace in the parsonage. Being a Californian, he had built even fewer coal fires than I had. But finally he devised a system: just place the hose of the tank vacuum cleaner on the exhaust end, and use it like a bellows to get the coals red hot. That worked fine—on weekends.

But on weekdays while Lee was gone, I struggled with little success, and at one of the country church board meetings, I happened to mention that I just couldn't keep a fire going.

"Easy—throw a bucket of gas on it," replied one staunch, straight-faced member. "That'll sure get it going," added another. I should have been cued in by the round of laughter, but my survival instincts and the need to keep our baby warm had heard only the method.

Several weeks later I was working valiantly over the old furnace. Nothing seemed to keep the coals burning, and the house was settling into the low sixties in the early afternoon. Then I remembered—the bucket of gas! The baby was asleep, the gas station just a block and a half away. I could get there and back before Mark woke up. Galvanized bucket in hand, I started down the street—right past the porch of the lady of communion-tray fame.

"Where're you going?"

"To get a bucket of gas."

"What do you need that for?"

"I can't get the furnace going and one of the men told me. . . ."

How I thank God for putting that woman on her front porch that day! Not only did she stop me from getting the gas, she taught me a lesson in gullibility, helped me get a fire going, and called the president of the church trustees to order the furnace converted from coal to oil. Of course we couldn't afford the oil bill on our $1,800 a year and lived mostly in the kitchen during the really cold days, but not all blessings need to be perfect.

While I was trying to keep warm, Lee was trying to be a minister. This meant he must preach—not just once, but twice every Sunday. And since he was a student pastor and away at school all week, it also meant that all the meetings for both churches, as well as the services, had to be held on weekends. Result? Very little time together. But first, let me tell you about Lee's preaching.

People sometimes compared him to Peter Marshall, a major preacher of that time, so, like any flattered young preacher, he began to borrow some of Marshall's sermons. This ended fairly soon, however, when one woman recognized a sermon and told him she had come to hear Lee Truman, not Peter Marshall. Then he was really on his own—with a little help from his seminary professors.

Lee owned one suit—the gray one he had bought when we were married. He also had only a couple of ties, and his favorite was red, with which he wore red socks (and a white shirt!). That's how he was dressed the first time a seminary professor came to critique him—unannounced, of course. When Lee returned to seminary the following week, the sermon evaluation was waiting in his mailbox. Across the top was scrawled, in appropriate red ink: "Somebody tell this boy what to wear in the pulpit!" That's when we decided that a pulpit robe was in order.

There was no money for a ready-made robe, so I bought a pattern and began the construction. The problem was that the church people didn't believe their pastor should wear a robe. It smacked of the Roman Catholic church (the one around the corner), and so did the two candles Lee had dared to place on the altar. A robe was an insult to their Protestant instincts.

So while I sewed dozens of tiny shoulder pleats by hand, Lee tried to figure out what else he could wear. From some source, he came up with a dark-blue suit. He also had a pair of blue slacks—a sort of bright deep teal blue. And he had a big wedding coming up.

Weddings had to be planned for weekends, too, and this one was on Friday evening. Providing Lee's timing was not disturbed, he would arrive home just in time to change clothes and walk into the church to begin the ceremony.

Friday traffic was a little heavier than usual that week, and Lee came rushing in the back door, calling for me to find his ritual book. We could see that the church must be full—cars were parked everywhere. He took the stairs three at a time and in minutes was back, gathering up the book and license, running out the door toward the church.

Everyone was there—from the town banker to the head of the volunteer fire department and the president of the Lion's Club. Lee took a deep breath, walked to his place behind the altar rail, and signaled the organist to begin the wedding march. The members of the bridal party took their places. All was in order.

Well, almost. Halfway through the ceremony, the bride began to sob. Louder and louder. Finally she caught her breath and wailed, "Has anybody got a handkerchief?" A quick search produced one, whereupon she blew her nose soundly, while everyone waited for the wedding to continue.

But in looking for the handkerchief, Lee had seen it: with the whole town looking on, he was wearing a dark-blue coat, teal-blue pants, and red socks! That did it! Even the protestors agreed that, at least for this particular minister, a robe might be a good thing.

<h2 style="text-align:center">4</h2>

The robe marked a new era. At first, it signified a search for dignity. It seemed to Lee that since he was over six feet tall, he must look rather awkward when he knelt on one knee. It also seemed that his feet were apt to become tangled up in the hem of the robe when he stood up from that one-knee position. (Today the hem is sewn in with a tight machine stitch!) So he began to practice kneeling on both knees at the same time, doing a deep-knee bend all the way to the floor. This way, his shoulders stayed straight and the robe fell evenly, out of the way of his heels.

The Communion table in the town church had its own unique shape. The top was ordinary enough, but the lower shelf, the bracing shelf, was just that—a bracing shelf, with its center curved inward to appear more artfully designed. On most Sundays, the two candles and the offering plates sat on top of the table. On Communion Sundays, however, the offering plates had to sit on the bracing shelf so that there was room on top for the Communion trays.

It was on a Communion Sunday that Lee chose to use his new kneeling technique. By this time he had served Communion often enough to be comfortable with the service, and all was progressing well. After a brief sermon, he called on the ushers to receive the "tithes and offerings." They did, and he did. Taking the plates from the ushers, he placed them side by side on the lower shelf.

The liturgy followed. We reached the point where the minister faces the altar table that holds the Communion elements and kneels to pray. This was what Lee had been practicing for! I watched his shoulders glide evenly down, proud of him for wanting this detail to be right. (Oh, how *young* we were!) Then it happened.

Both knees arrived at exactly the same time, catching the edges of both offering plates. They clattered to the floor. Nickles, dimes, quarters, half-dollars, and pennies rolled in all directions across the bare wood behind the altar rail. Lee lost his place in the liturgy. And for the rest of the service, as he walked back and forth serving the communicants, the whole church was aware of the crunching of money under his size-twelve feet. Humility strikes in the oddest ways. . . .

By the time the seminary professor came the next year, Lee was beginning to feel that he had some of the tough parts of preaching under control. He had somehow survived a whole year—and so had the congregations. This time there was advance warning that the professor would arrive on Reformation Sunday. Unfortunately, there was also a party Saturday night at the country church.

That year the country church had launched a building project. They needed a social hall and church school space, so on weekends, Lee and the members had come together to work. Gradually, a modest cement block building grew up beside the white-steepled church, with camraderie and laughter a part of the mortar. Now, after the last day's work, we celebrated with a potluck supper and square dance that went on till almost midnight.

Reformation Sunday dawned bright and early. We were neither. We struggled to some degree of alertness, aware that weekend living was beginning to take its toll. Lee was nervous, since he hadn't been able to get his sermon into good shape. Just in case his voice acted up, he went over to the church and placed a pitcher of water and a glass on the inside shelf of the pulpit.

Donning his robe gave him confidence—at least he was dressed right (the armor of God?). The professor was there on schedule, sitting in the last pew, center. Just before the sermon, Lee did what he always did. He slid his hymnbook into the pulpit shelf—knocked over the pitcher, and found himself standing in a puddle during the whole sermon. And what a sermon! He threw in everything he had ever learned about the Reformation. Martin Luther never had it so good! I relaxed in the pew and admired my husband.

The next Friday, I waited eagerly for the fine report he would surely bring home. But the eagerness I had anticipated was missing when he walked in. Silently Lee handed me the paper, like a schoolboy facing his mother. Written prominently under "Sermon Preparation" were these words: Don't over-prepare!

We laughed all weekend.

## 5

I was born and bred a city girl—with five locks on every outside door—so the first Tuesday when Lee drove off to seminary leaving Mark and me alone in the old creaky house, a cold chill crept through my psyche.

I could cope with stubborn furnaces, soon learned to conduct a Wednesday night prayer meeting, was pretty good at house cleaning and mothering, but going to bed alone in an empty house in a strange town was a full cup of fear for me—one of many cups I could not free myself of.

Even though the people became names, and the names became friends and neighbors, my nights increased in terror. Locked in our bedroom with our six-month-old child, I would doze off exhausted, only to jump awake at the slightest strange sound. In an ancient house, strange sounds are the order of the night.

As the weeks passed, small events increased my fear. The phone rang in the wee hours, but by the time I ran downstairs to answer it, the caller had hung up. All during another night I lay terrified, listening to an erratic sound as if someone were dragging a knife across a screen. The next morning I searched until I found the guilty screen—and cut off the loose wire that had immobilized me as the wind dragged it back and forth.

On one particularly moonless night, I thought I heard a baby's cry. The wailing grew louder as the night progressed, and finally I realized it was coming from an old abandoned well behind the house. Convinced that a child had fallen in, I called my closest neighbor out of bed to help investigate. Carefully removing the splintered boards that almost covered the top, he shone his powerful flashlight into the dark hole. Two gleaming green eyes glared up at us—a kitten, caught at the bottom of the well. I spent the rest of the night planning the cover that must be put over that gaping watery darkness, lest my own baby tumble in unobserved.

Then came the storms. I love thunder and lightening. But I was not prepared for hurricanes, blizzards, or fog that hid the earth. The highest branches of the trees would brush the ground in the furious wind, the walls of the old house would sway, and the loose kitchen wallboard would flap noisily. And my soul would shiver.

Each weekend we tried to find time for us. Late one Friday night, after many weeks of aloneness, I called a meeting to tell Lee some important people were waiting for him at the parsonage. They were named Mark and Ruth. When he was home I felt secure. On Tuesday morning as the car disappeared, I began to descend; by Thursday night I was on the bottom, struggling to survive just one more day until he returned. It was on such a Thursday night that fear almost destroyed us.

I had gone to bed early. Because one of our members had charged me with not trusting God to conquer my fear—and I knew he was right—I had moved Mark into the next room. Now when he needed me in the night, I had to overcome my fear, get up and move around. I also had to leave my bedroom door open so I could hear his cry. As was my pattern, that night I read until my eyes would no longer stay open, then dropped into a troubled sleep.

A footstep jerked me awake, shaking. I listened. Steps were coming through the dining room, heavy steps only a man would make. Quietly I slid the drawer open and, commanding my hand to stop trembling, took out the loaded .38 revolver Lee had put there.

The intruder was at the bottom of the stairs. I moved along the wall until I could just peer out the bedroom door without being seen. The gun was braced against the doorjamb, cocked, my nervous finger on the trigger. Breathless with fear, I waited as the person began to climb the stairs, not knowing whether I could shoot, but realizing I must protect our baby.

Suddenly the moonlight broke through the trees and silhouetted the familiar figure of my husband against the staircase window. He had come home late after Thursday classes because of an unexpected Friday holiday—and I had almost shot him.

I cried hysterically as he held me close. Quietly, he unloaded the gun. Both of us were forced to face my worst enemy—not an intruder, but fear. Fear was eating away our joy, destroying our inner peace. It waited each night to kill our hope for the future.

We put the gun away. We prayed. We survived. And gradually I outgrew my fear. The old house became my friend. But you can bet I made up my mind to find a way to travel back and forth with my husband just as soon as married-student housing was available and we could find a way to afford it!

6

Meanwhile, Lee decided the time had come to paint the church. There was enough rivalry between the Presbyterians and Methodists to convince our board that this action not only was important, but should be carried out with haste.

The only problem was money. (Sometimes I think that really *is* the only problem!) There was enough to buy the paint—maybe—but certainly not enough to hire a painter. In fact, there weren't any local painting contractors who could handle such a big job. Painters would have to come from one of the nearest large cities, a devastating expense in itself.

So Lee proposed a bargain. If the church board would buy the paint, he would do the work during his summer vacation. He had already secured the volunteer fire department's promise of their extension ladder to reach the steeple, and besides, a young man had volunteered to help when he could. (Lee had assumed that would be most of the time. . . . Wrong!)

The board took a deep communal breath. I was never sure whether it was because they had to catch their breath after such a long discussion, or whether the cost of paint and the image of their minister painting the church was overwhelming, but the board members voted to buy the paint. And they all agreed to help. Well, some of them agreed to help . . . actually, one or two mumbled something about finding time, maybe.

Preparation day began, and so did Lee. Just Lee. Donning his oldest jeans and a T-shirt, he started to scrape—a big church with a basement, an educational wing, and a steeple whose top was sixty feet from the ground. By the end of the first day he had cleaned only a small spot, but he was undaunted.

Next day he picked up the scraper again. About noon he decided that just maybe Lee was going to do this job all alone, and in that case he would need some power tools. A trip to a neighboring town produced a sander and spray-paint compressor. Two days faded into three, then four.

On the fifth day, the husband of the woman who kept me

from burning down the house came over to check the progress. He often checked things—such as what we were throwing away out of the garage—and today checking was his only interest—to see what progress Lee was making. He stood observing, smoking his pipe and making comments about places Lee had missed where the paint might not stick if the surface weren't completely clean.

At last he turned to leave. He knocked out his pipe against the cornerstone, stuck it in his shirt pocket, and commented, "It sure is good to see a minister working. I always did say the preacher is the highest paid man by the hour in this town!" Lee's anger increased his progress that day. . . .

Finally it was time to buy the paint—a forty-five gallon barrel of sparkling white. Then the fun began. Every sweep of the sprayer brought new life to the old boards. Cars slowed down to see how the job was coming. Sometimes a voice would call out, "Good work, preacher!"

Actually Lee had made more progress than one could see driving by, since he had practiced with the spray gun on the back and the side next to the house. The mistakes were less obvious there. By the time he moved to the street side and the front of the church, he was a professional painter minus union card.

Two young men began to come around to watch. Lee had seen them racing their cars at the local track. They asked about the steeple. How was he going to reach the back? It was obvious that even with the fireladder extension fully open, the back of the steeple would evade the spray. They also noticed that Lee was working alone.

Lee had been worrying about the same thing. How *would* he paint the back of that steeple? There was only one way: lean the ladder against the steeple, with one leg of the ladder locked on each side of the roof peak. The problem was how to get the ladder onto the roof, and then keep it from falling off as he worked.

By now it was clear that a major concern of many of the church people was not the completion of the painting, but the impropriety surrounding the reputation of the painter! He had made the mistake, for example, of going to the post office in his speckled jeans and T-shirt. By the end of that day someone had managed to tell him that the minister never goes into any of the businesses in town without a suit and tie. . . . And word was getting out that the minister *was* the painter. It would help if the whole thing were finished so it could be forgotten.

But their problems were not Lee's. In fact, they barely touched his consciousness, so intent was he on making the Methodist church the most attractive building around. People would surely flock to an attractive building. And besides, the painting was just the beginning. He had plans no one had even dreamed of . . . yet!

And this first big dream was not quite finished—there was still the back side of the steeple. If he used one ladder to get up on the roof, he could hook a rope around a vent pipe and pull the other ladder up. He was struggling with this task when his two watchers arrived—this time they offered to help. Not only did they help get the ladder onto the roof, but they climbed up and held it—one on each leg—while Lee leaned first to one side and then the other to paint the steeple.

The church was finished—painted from top to bottom—by the minister and two fellows from the race track. And the people began to talk about how beautiful *their* church looked.

However—the parsonage next door looked dreadful by comparison. There was really nothing else to do. Once you've painted a church, a two-story house is nothing, right? Just twelve more gallons of sparkling white, a few windows masked, and voila!—the parsonage glistens like the church. The work went quickly, but the longer Lee painted, the more he thought about the roof.

The shingles were dry and had begun to twist. Oil would renew them. So with the whole house sparkling white, Lee decided to give the roof a heavy coat of linseed oil shingle paint before he returned the compressor. Bright green. Like the trees around it. He would be careful so not too much would get on the house. . . .

And he was careful. And fast. And the shingles were very slippery. Suddenly Lee lost his footing and began sliding down the high peaked roof so marvelous for shedding snow in New Jersey winters. As he was about to go over the edge, he threw an arm around the chimney. He held, but a large section of the chimney didn't. It rained bricks. Later, he carefully stacked them back in place. Somebody else could worry about the mortar.

It was time for Lee to put back on his suit and tie!

7

In order to afford that suit and tie, plus seminary tuition, I took a job teaching seventh grade in the local elementary school. Mark was now toddling everywhere, so we found a beautiful grandmother who came each morning to tidy the house and care for him. On $1800 a year, we had a housekeeper—paid out of my salary, of course. And we've never been able to afford one since!

Lee was getting used to being a minister. He had survived his first ecumenical Thanksgiving service. By some mysterious rotation, it had fallen his lot to preach the first Thanksgiving after our arrival. For weeks he worked on his sermon, looked up illustrations, pored over Scripture, prayed. The day before the service he paced the floor, rehearsing the words he had written so carefully. Actually, he was scared to death.

But he trusted God and preparation to bring him through, and it worked. He preached eloquently. As people were filing out the door, a little woman from the Foursquare Church approached him, patted his arm, and asked, "Reverend Truman, could I have a copy of that sermon, or did it come from the heart?" Lee never could remember his answer.

He would never forget the next year, however, the year everyone came to our church—the newly painted one—and with the sanctuary packed to the doors, he forgot to take the offering! Fortunately (or unfortunately), these events only happened once a year. . . .

Not only were we getting used to the ministry, but the people were getting used to us. They had discovered a stock excuse for the indiscretions of New Jersey decorum which we sometimes committed (about once a week): Lee was from California. Everybody knows that Californians are a little different from everybody else. Besides, he was just a *student* pastor.

The country church had a special way of loving us. After the service when we climbed in the car, there would be a bag of potatoes, or corn, or fresh green vegetables. Or someone would invite us to farm-cooked meals—often with oysters on the half shell. Clams and oysters are a great delicacy in that part of the country, but eating them raw almost undid my Christianity. Still, one learns to accept blessings, whatever shape they're in—even raw.

Lee was still traveling the hundred miles each Tuesday morning to school. He was studying Barth, Tillich, and Niebuhr. At home, I was leading Bible study on Mark, Matthew, and John. He wrote papers on "The Teleological Suspension of the Ethical" and came home to preach about the love of God to people who often had not finished high school.

They all knew about the love of God, though—especially the saintly founder of the country community. (It was at his house that I almost lost my oysters!) Gently he instructed Lee that New Jersey is not a part of New England, though he could see why a Californian might think so. When the church door opened, he was there. When something needed doing, he was there—helping, and often paying for it. When Lee preached poorly, he found a good point and praised him for it.

His death taught us how to mourn. As the casket was lowered into the ground in the cemetery beside the church, the tears flowed unchecked from the eyes of minister and congregation alike. A giant had fallen, and in the falling had scattered fragments of God's love into every grieving heart. And we all grew.

Maybe it was because of that love that Lee began to think about lighting the steeples of both churches—one to shine in the absolute darkness of the country sky, one to illuminate the town. The town church was, after all, on the main thoroughfare, the first prominent building one saw after turning off the highway. And the Presbyterian church was talking about lighting their building, now that ours was so much more attractive.

That was all it took! When the Methodist board found out that the Presbyterian church might be lighted, the matter was settled. Money was available—to buy the materials. The labor? Well, after all, it was the preacher's idea. . . .

This time some of the men came around to help. The standards were set in the ground, and someone was there to hold the ladder while Lee swung by a belt from the steeple to set the lights pointing toward the new cross that had been mounted on top. (Shades of the Roman Catholic church around the corner!) The church glowed, and so did the people.

But each time Lee climbed up that steeple, he found himself eyeing the bell, a one-and-a-half ton beauty, laid on its side and rigged so that only the clapper moved to call people to worship. Such a beautiful bell could be heard for miles if it were hanging free. So one Saturday afternoon Lee climbed up inside the belfry and, ever so gently, undid the cables and turnbuckles, allowing the bell to slide into its cradle in a hanging position.

Sunday dawned especially clear the next day—perfect weather for carrying sound on a gentle breeze. People were beginning to arrive, walking to church from homes and cars, when Lee gave the first pull on the bellrope. The bell began to ring. Suddenly, above the clarion tones, we heard a frantic voice: "Stop! Stop!"

The board president was running as fast as his short legs could carry him, coat and tie flying. Lee handed the rope to an usher and hurried to meet him.

"Look . . . ," the man gasped, completely winded. There, for all to see, the *whole steeple* was swaying from side to side with every tug on the rope. This marked the beginning of wisdom. It is wise to ask *why* things are the way they are. Maybe—just maybe—there's a reason!

For the next several weeks, Lee mulled over the problem of a bell too heavy for a steeple. What good is a church steeple that stands higher than anything else in town, if its bell can't be heard more than a half mile away? Sitting in class one day, he was suddenly aware of the campus chimes tolling the hour. That was it! Of course. A carillon!

"A what?" The incredulous response from the board was unanimous.

As if nothing had been said, Lee plunged on. He could buy an amplifier and a record player, rig a timer to the outfit and, for very little cost, play hymns every evening. People for miles around would identify the music with the Methodist church. It would be beautiful. On Sunday as the service was about to begin, a hymn would call the town to church. By the time the bell rang, everyone would be prepared for worship. And the steeple was high enough so that the sound would not bother the neighbors close to the building, since it would go over their heads.

His open-mouthed audience sat stunned. The painting, they had gone along with. Then the cross on top of the steeple—even if it did smack of Rome. The basement remodeling. The lights. To say nothing of the candles on the altar and the pulpit robe . . . and now he wanted a carillon.(How do you pronounce that?)

"I think we ought to do it."

Every head turned in perfect unison. It was the wealthiest woman in the church who had broken the silence.

Immediately the board president regained his composure. "Are there any objections?" Waiting scarcely a second for response, he pronounced it done. Then it was Lee's turn to sit with his mouth open!

Piece by piece the components came together until all was ready. The record player was housed in the study at the parsonage; the wires ran underground across the lawn, then up the steeple to the speakers. Each night at dusk, one hymn played. When the hymn ended, the needle sat in the groove of the record until the next evening. And new people began to come to the sparkling white church that glowed by day and by night, following the invitation of the music flowing from its steeple.

8

With the building in order and the pews filling every week, it was time to turn some attention to the inside of the parsonage. The kitchen wallboard was still flapping in the breeze, the dining-room floor needed a rug, some painting was desperately called for, and the living-room furniture was worn out.

The woman's society was in charge of the parsonage, and the woman across the street was the president (the communion-tray and gasoline woman). When the subject of redoing at least the kitchen was broached, it touched off discussions in and out of official meetings. Maybe they could just glue the wallboard back in place. No, they ought to put insulation in the walls and do it right. They could hire the local painter to do the cupboards—he was good, but expensive. They knew some people who were refurbishing their living room; perhaps their old furniture could be donated to the parsonage. And so it went. Finally they decided that while we were vacationing in California, they would fix up the house.

Meanwhile, the seminary had announced that more married-student housing would be available in the fall. We were thoroughly tired of living apart all week, and our son was missing contact with his father, so we put our name on the list. I applied for a teaching job in a town just five miles from the seminary, at three times the pay I was earning in our town. If I got the job we could afford the apartment. Nothing was definite when it was time to leave for California, so we said nothing to the board. After all, we had no intention of leaving our churches—we just wanted to travel back and forth *together*.

Word reached us in California that the apartment—and the job—were ours. I promptly wrote the principal in our town and resigned from teaching for the coming year. When we returned the following week, everybody knew all about our plans, and a special board meeting had been called.

"Why did you want the kitchen fixed when you're not even going to live here?" "We don't want our parsonage sitting empty all week!" "That makes you a part-time minister. . . . We're not used to that."

My mind whirled. The kitchen was their property. Shouldn't it be kept in good repair? And listen to them— arguing about *my* right to choose to live with my husband.

Don't they know how hard it is to be alone for two years? All they care about is the house! And how could Lee be a part-time minister simply because *I* travel back and forth? He'd *always* been a part-time minister—only now I wouldn't be there to hold Wednesday night prayer meeting at the house. . . . Then the voice of our wealthy parishioner broke through. She had been arguing most vehemently that someone should live in the parsonage, but she concluded with, "I've never spent a night alone in my life."

*They didn't know!* These people had lived in this town all their lives, protected, surrounded by family. Living alone, apart, was outside their experience. . . .

The country church laughed at the town church. "Tell you what, Ruth," one man said. "We'll let them keep the preacher, and *we'll* keep the preacher's wife!"

"It's just like them to worry about their house," said another. "You two ought to be together." But then they were used to a part-time minister: I *always* came and went with Lee, as far as the country church was concerned.

At last the board decided to keep us—even though they *had* redone the kitchen and no one would use it during the week.

It was beautiful. A new dinette table stood by the windows that overlooked the grove of oak and maple trees. Cabinets glistened. Walls were insulated. And I had polished the floor to a supershine. The "new" living-room furniture was scarcely worn—it was a great improvement. Only the rug secured for the dining room marred the appearance. It had been stored behind an outhouse. Thank heavens for dining-room tables that cover such stained blessings!

With that project finished, we began our year of commuting. So that I could report to work on Monday morning we left late Sunday evening, usually after a meeting, and came home after my school was out on Friday afternoon. Into this shorter weekend, all the same meetings and activities now had to be crammed . . . and we began to understand what they meant by a "part-time" minister. There really was a big difference between a minister who was available from Friday afternoon through Monday night, and one on our new schedule. And with the house locked all week, there was no one to consult with—even though it might be only the untrained wife!

We were still very young! Unfortunately, our car was not. Two hundred miles a week were beginning to show. Frequently Lee would have to take it apart on those short weekends. He was repairing a major problem one Saturday when a man in his thirties (*old* to us . . .) knocked at the front door. He wanted to see the minister, so I invited him in while I summoned Lee.

Car-working clothes are a lot like church-painting clothes. Blue jeans, covered this time with paint *and* grease, plus a T-shirt that appeared to be doubling as a wiping rag. Lee cleaned his hands as best he could (car grease doesn't give up easily) and greeted the man in the living room. For about twenty minutes they talked about cars. Finally, with note of exasperation (or was it desperation?), the visitor said, "I've really enjoyed talking with you, young man, but I came to see the minister. Is he here?" Then they started all over again. . . . Appearances can be deceiving.

I was enjoying teaching home economics and car pooling with two other seminary wives. But as winter deepened, the car became more obstinate. Finally, on a day I was to drive, it refused to start at all. Lee was in class; there was nothing to do but take another teacher's car. On the way to work that day, smarting from the humiliation of a car that wouldn't run, I saw the yellow convertible.

It sat on the showroom floor, looking for all the world like sunny California. We had been able to put some money aside from my new income and had even lucked out on a small stock market investment. When I finally got Lee to the dealer's showroom, I could tell by the way he walked around and around the car that he wanted it, too. Back and forth we went every weekend, riding in our failing Plymouth, talking about the convertible. Our friends dubbed us crazy. No one buys a convertible in New Jersey. . . . Besides, it's winter. They were right on both counts, but come June and graduation, we would be moving back to California where the sun always shines.

We bought the yellow convertible in the middle of February. The next week a blizzard struck, the trunk froze solid, and snow drifted clear up to the windows. . . . For ten straight weekends, the weather was so bad that we drove peering out the side window to see the white line at the edge of the highway. Blizzards. Fog. Rain. We laughed with our friends as they teased us about the convertible, but we talked more about California every week. For us, the top was already rolled back and the sun was shining in.

9

Our commuter status never sat comfortably with the town church. About mid-year our neighbor, the women's-society-president-parsonage-chairperson (to use a current term), told us she would need to get into the house during the week; would we please give her our key? When asked why, she simply said it was time to "check things." Assuming she needed to report to the parsonage committee, we gave her the key.

When we arrived home the following Friday night, Lee went across the street to pick up the key. She handed it to him with the words, "You won't have to loan it to me again. I had one made so I could get in any time."

By the time my even-tempered husband had reached our back door, he was livid. How dare she presume that she could come into *our* home any time she pleased? What kind of privacy rights did a minister have? Was it our house, or wasn't it? He simply wouldn't be calmed.

Upstairs putting Mark to bed, I could hear Lee banging on something below, then silence. He was gone. Minutes later, he came back smiling.

"What did you do?"

"I took the lock off and gave it to her."

"You *what*?" I was incredulous!

"I took the lock off and gave it to her. I told her that since she had the key, she might as well have the lock, too, and I would put a new one on our door." He smiled triumphantly.

I was horrified. You just didn't *do* that to the women's society president and get away with it. But the lock was gone, and the next day a new one took its place. Then the strangest thing happened: she never mentioned it—not to me, not to anybody. And neither did we. . . .

But to leave a house unattended all week with the key in one's pocket is actually not too bright, as we were to discover some weeks later.

The carillon had been well received in the town and the surrounding areas. Lee had gradually increased the volume to a three-mile range. The church was proud to be the source of eventide hymns. Each week before we left, Lee would set up the equipment for the coming week. And each day it would perform mightily on cue. Till that fateful Thursday.

At its usual time, the record began to play. The hymn drifted over the wintry landscape, adding its secure touch to the rooted lives of the townspeople. It played to the end. When the needle caught in the groove and the timer failed to shut off the equipment, the alarming realization dawned: the parsonage was locked; the controls were inside; no one had a key. And for three miles in every direction, the Methodist church carillon was playing "Ka-thunk, ka-thunk, ka-thunk. . . ."

Frantically the trustees pried at the windows, to no avail. The doors refused all skeleton keys. They would have to break a window. . . . Then someone remembered the cellar. Throwing back the outside cellar doors, they almost fell down the steps in their hurry to stop the noise, which by now was causing telephones to ring in all their homes. "Shut that damn thing off!" A skeleton key slid into the lock, and with sighs of relief they all raced upstairs to throw the switch. The next week, the trustee president asked for a key to the parsonage—for emergency use only. We agreed without comment.

Spring came, and we were ready. Our tow-headed Mark was running everywhere—especially to see the commuter train go through town twice daily. (Lee said it was the only thing in this town that went through without him pushing it.) Mark was approaching his third birthday; it was time to enlarge our family. Lee would be graduating, and the California bishop had promised us an appointment in June. So before long, almost four of us were commuting.

And Lee began to build our covered wagon for the trek westward.

## 10

Lee had never built a trailer before. He had built racing cars, worked on heavy construction equipment, and lived in a house trailer. So . . .

Aerodynamic, it wasn't. In fact, we dubbed it The Boxcar. It was meant to hold all our now expanded goods, so the sides went straight up almost seven feet and the floor was six feet wide. To class it up, Lee painted it to match our convertible—half yellow, half white, over its twelve-foot length. Covered wagons had nothing on us!

People began to drop by to watch the progress as the weekends marched inevitably toward graduation. Each board added to its height added to the sadness we felt from these dear people who, after all, had loved us. But we could think only about our trip to the promised land of desert, sea, and mountain—every climate one could desire within an hour or two of home. Sunday sermons had an influx of California illustrations. In his mind, Lee was already dipping in the waves of the Pacific, traversing the slopes of Mammoth Mountain, camping in the midst of the Sequoias. Later he would tell Californians about New Jersey, but right now he could only look West.

Graduation day arrived. Mark and I watched proudly as Lee received his divinity degree. With the ceremonies completed, we packed everything from the apartment into The Boxcar and, for the last time, drove to South Jersey—to our glistening white church, to the last service in town and in country, to farewell receptions at both.

What a weekend! The trailer was filled to its roof—seminary papers, new concordances, baby furniture, household goods, TV. When we finally locked the tailgate, there was not an empty inch.

Sunday's dawn could have been a California morning. Late spring flowers scented the air, warmed by a sparkling sun in a deep blue sky. We were to meet with conference officials in

California on Thursday, so our plan was to pick up the trailer and leave as soon as the country church service was over.

Both churches were full. Hugs. Backslapping. Parting words. Our first inkling of the unusual came when we were halfway back to town. On the road behind us we could see a steady procession of cars. As we backed the convertible into place in front of the waiting trailer, we noticed that the town church parking lot was full. It should have been empty, since the service there had ended almost two hours earlier. It looked as though no one had left.

After making one last check of the trailer connections and setting our ice chest, our son, and ourselves into place, we eased along the gravel drive behind the church and onto the street. As we approached the corner of Main Street, we saw the people—town and country mixed together—standing on each side of the street almost out to the highway—waving—calling goodbye—crying. Our people. God's people. Forever.

Lee broke the silence of our tears. "The mechanic who checked the trailer hitch yesterday told me that if going to California is God's will for us, we'd have smooth sailing; and if it isn't, we'd have trouble all the way." We laughed and began to talk of our bright new future.

Twelve miles out of town, Lee pulled over to the side of the highway to investigate a strange sound coming from the trailer. The tires were leaning precariously toward the center. The axle had cracked. It took two tow trucks to lift The Boxcar off its frame and four hours to weld new units into place. The sun was low in the sky when we set out again for California.

"God's will? Or trouble all the way?" My words hung unanswered as the miles began to disappear beneath our covered wagon.

A few weeks later lightning struck the church steeple and wiped out the carillon . . . and nobody knew how to fix it.

# The Middle, First Half

California, here we come—ready or not!

## 1

We drove all night. At least Lee did. I made Mark a bed in the back seat and propped my own head against the vibrating window, exhausted. Some time during the early morning hours we switched and Lee slept, but since I had never pulled a trailer before, our speed slowed considerably. Alarmed that we might not arrive at our new annual conference on schedule, Lee took the wheel again as Monday's sun began its course.

The uneventful day calmed our spirits. Calling on hopes and dreams buoyed our tired bodies. A picnic lunch, a romp with Mark, and the promise of a shower and good bed in St. Louis brought us to mid-day slightly ahead of schedule. Around three o'clock Lee's body rebelled, so again I began to drive while he and Mark slept. One hundred miles to St. Louis and rest. . . .

The terrain began to change, as did the sun. Clouds gathered over the road ahead. The highway climbed and dipped over rolling hills, and four lanes dissolved into two. Misty rain wet the windshield and left the asphalt oil-glazed and puddled. Cars were lined up behind us, but there was no letup in the oncoming traffic, and no place for passing or moving over. My foot pushed the accelerator as hard as I dared. Fifty. Fifty-five. The driver behind us kept swerving toward the middle to check for a passing space. A sign flitted into my side vision: CURVE/HILL.

The curve was sharp, the hill steep. My braking was too abrupt for the wet road. Before I could comprehend the meaning of the tugs on the steering wheel, the trailer began to whip. Lee sat straight up, screaming, "Pull with it!" But all I could do was hang on for dear life, not having the strength to fight the weight of our loaded Boxcar. Oncoming cars stopped. The tailgate flew open (God lightens our load in mysterious ways). Our belongings started flying, first to one side of the road, then the other. A final swing of the trailer spun us around, and pointed uphill into a bank, we stopped. The sound of spilling fluid! Lee grabbed Mark and across the wet pavement we ran, away from the inevitable explosion. Nothing happened. Then we saw the water from our overturned ice chest running out the open back door.

We were alive. No one was hurt. There was a single fold in the fender of our shiny new convertible. But for fifty yards in every direction, our worldly goods lay in the mud and rain. "Trouble all the way . . ." went through my mind as we turned the car around and began to toss our soggy belongings into the trailer. People helped us until the road was passable, and then we darted back and forth with an armload whenever we could. Our prized TV rested facedown across the road on the edge of a forty-foot drop, its knobs sheared smooth. (It worked for years afterward!) Lee's seminary notes, so carefully filed, were lying in damp piles everywhere; his new concordances were covered with mud.

"We'll straighten it out in St. Louis." Shoes, suitcases, toys, books. The Salvation Army wouldn't have picked up our distressed load! It was well past dark when we pulled in beside the first motel vacancy sign on the outskirts of St. Louis. We had traveled far enough for Monday.

Rain was still falling Tuesday morning. Sorting the contents of the trailer would have to wait for a sunnier climate. We drove a long day, fell into an exhausted sleep, and awoke Wednesday behind schedule. No time to straighten the trailer and make it to conference in Redlands. Our original Thursday morning plan had been to stop with relatives in Los Angeles, unpack and leave Mark, then go on to Redlands. Now we would have to travel directly there, check into a motel, and do our best to find our good clothes.

As Lee drove, I checked the map for a more direct route. There was a major highway up through the mountains that would save many miles. There was one large town—Jerome—and many smaller places to refuel. So we headed across the Arizona desert for the junction. The new road began to climb steadily. The heat indicator also climbed as the car struggled with its unruly load, but we were confident we could stop in Jerome to cool the motor. With the top down, we were keenly aware of the burning sun.

Up on the hill sat the town. When we passed the city-limits sign, our curiosity was piqued—such a small population for so many buildings. Then we realized that nothing seemed to be open, few people were around, and the weathered structures looked deserted. Jerome—Lee remembered then!—was a famous ghost town where the undermined buildings were slowly sliding down the mountain. As if on cue, the transmission also began to slip.

Upward through Jerome we went, up, up. "If the transmission can just make it to the top of the grade," Lee reasoned, "it will cool off and we can still get to conference late today." Needless to say, our shortcut was not. Finally a shuddering effort brought our overheated automobile to a halt. There was nothing to do but sit at the side of the road while it cooled. Time for another picnic. Mark thought it was great fun. . . .

As the sun was setting in the still elusive West, we finally came to a real town. Lee went to find a telephone. We were still many hours from our destination.

But saving grace was at work. The conference board would meet with us in special session on Friday, but no later than two o'clock, since their final adjournment was at three.

Just before noon on Friday, the palm-lined streets of Redlands came into view. We stopped at the first motel. Full. And the next. And the next. "Don't you know there's two thousand people in town for the Methodist Conference? There's not a place to be had." No room at the inn. . . .

"Wait—maybe they can put you up over at the Wisahikon Inn," the motel clerk added, looking at our child, our weary faces, hearing our story. Perhaps he saw the slight bulge that was beginning to fill my lap. He picked up the phone.

"Only a maid's room, will that do?" Would it! We drove our dented dusty convertible with its matching muddy Boxcar into the inn parking lot amid Cadillacs and Continentals. (It just happened to be the place the elite stayed and we've never stopped there since. . . .) No time to worry about that. We needed a telephone, a shower, an iron. With the board informed that we were in town and would arrive just as soon as we could change clothes, we searched through the trailer for the cases that held suit, good dress, shoes . . . that were mud-free—and in my case, that I could zip up. Our fourth family member was more prominent than I had realized.

At one o'clock we climbed the steps of the music building at the University of Redlands, conference headquarters. Lee looked fine in his gray suit, and I had found a dress with a jacket that covered the unzippable zipper. Only one thing marred our poise: Lee's shoes. His dress shoes were nowhere to be found. There was nothing to do but wear the ones he'd been driving in—the same brown moccasins all speckled green and white that he had worn when he painted the church.

"What will you tell them?"

"What else? That I painted the church in them."

A gracious woman met us at the top of the stairs and escorted Mark and me into a small room to wait. Lee went through the door marked Board of Ministry.

Time almost stopped. My mind was in the boardroom, even while I made small talk with my hostess. She said she was the wife of the chairman of the board—I called myself back to attention. . . . At last the door opened and I was asked to come in.

Fifteen or twenty men, impeccably dressed in suits, white shirts, and dark ties, sat in a semicircle, with Lee in his gray suit and paint-covered shoes sitting opposite—alone. I took the obvious unoccupied chair next to him. Questions began to fill the room. Somehow, I answered. The accident—the cracked axle—Jerome—the transmission. How did I feel after the ordeal? Fine. We were here now. I wondered why they didn't ask me about being a minister's wife or about serving a church. Instead, we laughed with joy at our journey's safe end. What did any of the troubles matter? It was only important that Lee be accepted into the conference.

"Are there any last questions?" the chairman asked. Silence.

Lee shifted in his chair. "If any of you are wondering about my shoes, I can explain. . . ." And he did.

A slight, freckled-faced man began to grin. "Well, I was just thinking that they looked a whole lot more comfortable than the ones I have on," he drawled. Laughter. Handshaking and words of welcome. God's will or not, we were in!

Later we would learn the board had decided that if we had been through all the experiences of that week and could still laugh, we would get through anything! It would be years before we knew what that meant. . . .


2


"Look. It's right here on the map. . . ." My finger traced a very crooked line running south on our California map.

No one needed to tell Lee it was crooked! We had been twisting and turning for more than an hour. Far to the left of our route, the map showed a perfectly straight highway connecting to another main artery that led directly to our destination. In miles, however, the road I had chosen was shorter. Shades of Jerome!

We rode in frustrated silence, our yellow Boxcar following obediently. There hadn't been a house or store for miles—just trees and winding asphalt. At least I had convinced Lee that we were heading in the right direction—more or less.

Mark had been fed and put to sleep on the back seat for an afternoon nap when the first house came into view. It was a boarded-up summer cottage, and many summers obviously had passed since its owners had visited. . . .

Mailboxes grouped alongside the road brought hope, especially since some were open. Somewhere, somebody—

maybe—lived in these wooded mountains. I remembered the face of the district superintendent (D.S.), as he earnestly explained that since we had arrived at conference so late, most of the churches already were assigned. He had fumbled with a book in his hand and looked off across the campus before he corrected himself. "All the churches have been assigned, actually, and I'm sure you'll have a good time in this little community." As he finished his brief description of the church, he thrust the book into Lee's hand: *Dig or Die, Brother Hyde*—something about a preacher who goes West to the end of the railroad and, unable to go farther, starts a church from nothing.

I shook the memory from my mind. After all, our assignment did have a building, a congregation, and a debt. On the other hand, the D.S. had seemed awfully anxious to end our conversation.

An old car flanked by piles of worn tires came into view, followed by a jumble of sheds, bed frames, broken chairs. The center shed seemed to be the house, from which tumbled dogs and waving children. Were cars so scarce on this road that each one rated a personal greeting?

Lee drove more slowly now, looking at the cottages, which appeared with increasing frequency. "We're coming to a junction, Ruth. Is that on the map?"

Triumph! The junction number told me we were right on target. "Turn right. It should take you into town." (How was I to know there wasn't one?)

We pulled into the graveled parking area of a fruit stand. A short muscular man eyed us suspiciously as Lee got out of the car and walked toward him. Three small heads appeared around the corner of the unpainted house nearby, and I felt another pair of eyes looking through the window. The man nodded in answer to Lee's questions, then pointed off to our right. A yell from the house sent the children scurrying inside. More words. Then Lee extended his hand to thank the man, who quickly wiped his own on his faded jeans before returning the gesture. Then, at last, he smiled.

Lee was *not* smiling as he walked back to the car. With death in his voice he said, "When we come to a basement building that looks like a big septic tank or an overgrown potato cellar, we've reached our church."

Forlornly, he turned the key. Yellow convertible and Boxcar edged onto the road. We had arrived, but we weren't sure where.

Less than a mile later, Lee suddenly jammed on the brakes. "Oh my God! I think we just passed it!" Somehow he managed to back up the trailer till we were parked parallel to our new "church."

Nothing was visible but a twelve-foot cross and a sign that read METHUDIST CHURCH. For what seemed a million years, we sat in stunned silence. I looked at Lee. He must have been looking at God. Neither of us could move.

The shock easing, we finally got out, walked to the far edge of the road, and peered over the embankment. There it was, just as the fruit-stand man had said—the potato cellar!

Recovering our senses, we scrambled down the weed-covered bank (we didn't know about the rattlesnakes then) and tried all three doors. Of course they were locked. The windows were covered with frosted glass. But one thing was obvious. If we had come to work, there was work to do. Lee's construction eye measured the condition of the drive that dipped dangerously onto the church property. Weather streaks stained the concrete-block building; its tarpaper roof had curled. So had Lee's spirits.

"We have to go, Lee. Remember the committee said they'd wait for us in front of the postoffice." (They could have said store, gas station, or icehouse. They were all one—and the only ones in "town".)

Back in the car, with Mark wide awake, we drove through our new community: cottages, grazing land, a schoolhouse, a pond. And then Perkins' Store—the town! A smiling face and waving hand hailed us. My excitement at seeing our new house fought then with what I heard: "Would you mind staying in a member's house till we can find a place for you? When the last minister left, he gave up the lease on his house without telling us, and we really don't have anyplace else to put you. . . ."

The words jumbled together in my tired brain. First no

church, now no house! *Dig or Die, Brother Hyde* was making more sense all the time.

### 3

For a month we lived in someone else's home. We used their towels, looked at their family pictures, wondered what kind of people they were. We ate from their plates and cooked with their pots and pans. And waited. The Boxcar sat on the edge of a gravel roadway, each passing car leaving another layer of fine dust on all our belongings. But many of the cars stopped—to deliver a cake or casserole, to say hello, to see how we were doing.

Shock behind him, Lee quickly sized up the church situation. There was a small room designated as an office, but there was no office furniture or typewriter. There *was* an ancient mimeograph, a main hall, furnace closet, kitchen, and two bathrooms—soundproof enough to have pleased our New Jersey ladies. Church school classes met in the four corners of the hall, in the kitchen, and in the "office." The choir boasted robes and twelve members. Most important of all, there were about fifty people who were determined to build a church in this mountain community.

The first Sunday, we watched as church school classes ended and the slatted wooden pews were quickly pushed into place for worship. Flowers fit for the finest cathedral appeared on the altar. A young man carefully lit the two candles. Ushers welcomed people at the doors. Whole families took their places together, often filling a pew. Then the pianist sat down at the old upright, the choir processed from the kitchen, and by the time Lee's black robe disappeared through the kitchen door at the end of the service, I could tell he had a love affair going.

The next week the widow of the beloved founding pastor took me aside. "I have two pieces of advice to give you," she confided. "First, buy a pair of jeans and wear them most of the time. And second, when you see someone coming, hide your dirty dishes in the oven."

I was speechless! In the Midwest where I grew up, no wife of a minister would have been caught dead—or alive, for that matter—in a pair of jeans, and some even frowned on slacks as "men's apparel." And hide the dishes? The very idea! Either people accepted us as honest human beings who usually have dirty dishes after we eat, or they needn't bother to come! On that last item I was right. But on the first? We were soon to discover we were in Wyatt Earp country, and Lee, with his construction background, probably was going to fit in a lot better than I.

Besides, I wasn't fitting into anything anymore. I longed for my sewing machine so I could make some maternity clothes, but it was somewhere in the trailer. Lee finally dug out his typewriter to make a bulletin, but each forage into The Boxcar left things in worse condition. We worried that the people in whose house we were living would be home soon, and what then?

With three days to spare, the committee called. They had found a house. Well actually, they had twisted the arm of a short dentist into renting the church his summer home. We knew he was short because Lee could stand up straight in only two rooms. The house had a marvelous view of the valley. It also had unvented heaters that couldn't be left on at night for fear of asphyxiation. A quaint kitchen eating area was built around a boulder with plants growing on its surface. Of course, the watering system for the plants dripped water from the rock to an open trough which exited the house through a fist-sized hole in the wall. Most convenient for lizards, scorpions, and other small critters seeking escape from the elements. . . .

The view was afforded by the placement of the house—three-quarters of the way up a mountain. To get to it, you put your car in low gear, got a racing start, then drove like mad to the top entrance of the circular drive, where you promptly applied the brakes so the car would stop about halfway around the drive, pointed slightly downhill in case the engine was being stubborn on a cold morning.

Unfortunately, we hadn't learned all this when we approached the hill with Boxcar in tow. The day was sunny, with fleecy white clouds adrift in deepest blue. Such excitement! Our own house at last! Confidently, we started up the hill in the yellow convertible. Lee easily made the sharp turn at the bottom, The Boxcar bouncing behind over gravel and rocks. Up, up—halfway up, that is. Wheels spinning, everything came to a halt. Mark and I walked the rest of the way while Lee tried again . . . and again. Finally, there was nothing to do but lighten the load, one armload at a time. Up and down the hill we trudged, piling our belongings on the large rocks that lined the driveway, until the almost empty trailer could at last be pulled into place beside the house.

By mid-afternoon we were moving numbly, carrying now-sorted piles one at a time into the house to newly lined shelves. The yard looked like a super garage sale, shaded from the July sun by . . .

Shaded? Oh no! I clicked into consciousness. Lee had gone down the hill to make a phone call. Mark was in bed, and there wasn't a neighbor in sight when the rain began to fall. Frantically I started grabbing piles, dumping them unceremoniously in blurred heaps on the porch and in the house. Soon Lee's hands joined mine, his errand cut short by raindrops. In minutes our careful day's work was undone. We sat exhausted on the one couch in the tiny living room, surrounded by soggy, muddy piles. For the second time, almost everything we owned had been rained on.

We might be there still but for the neighbor who came knocking at the door, dinner in hand. Just the other day when I was looking through a thirty-year-old mud-stained concordance, the aroma of that dinner drifted through my memory. Evelyn of Elf Cottage, thank you! Because of you, we survived.

## 4

Several weeks later Lee made his announcement about the ambulance. He had sat for an hour on the ground in front of Perkins' Store, cradling the head of a bleeding and bruised man whose Jeep had rolled over. We were forty miles from the nearest hospital, with a winding mountain road between us and emergency help. The people who gathered around the accident told Lee it was always this way. They gave what assistance they could, and then waited—unless they could get the injured person to the doctor on up the hill, and she wasn't always there. Today, for instance, was her day down in the city.

"I'm going to start an ambulance service, Ruth. As a church ministry. I think I can give the kids around here something to do besides terrorize the drivers on the mountain roads with their motorcycles." He leaned over and kissed me, giving my protruding tummy a pat. "Besides, when the time comes for my little girl to be born, I can take you to the hospital in style."

Two weeks later Lee had his ambulance—and the beginnings of The Bishop's Riders Club. To become a member, you had to be able to take an engine apart and repair it. The reward was to be trained as an attendant and ride in the ambulance (there were no paramedics then). Members who had safe driving records and had given help to people stranded on mountain roads won the privilege of wearing an insignia on the back of their motorcycle jackets. And of course they were expected to be in church most Sundays.

The ambulance was rented and frequently broke down, so there was a lot of training in motor rebuilding available. Word spread quickly among the mountain teenagers that there was something exciting to do at the Me*thod*ist church. (One of the first things Lee did was correct the spelling on the sign!) The boys came to join the club and the girls came to meet the boys (those were sexist days, you understand), and in no time we had a thriving youth group. After all, if you were at the church when the fire whistle blew a short and a long, you could be the first to jump aboard the ambulance for a wild, racing trip with full sirens screaming. And what stories there were to tell afterward: gory firsthand details of all the accidents in the area. Nothing could match the ambulance for excitement and ego building!

Cool fall nights had begun to turn the mountain trees into a blaze of color. With the colors came the city folk, out for Sunday drives and not used to mountain roads. The ambulance business was brisk, especially at Dead Man's

Curve, halfway up the mountain. The two-lane road had no barriers, and it was easy to misjudge speed and go over the edge. A winch and tow became regular equipment on the ambulance.

The Highway Patrol, pleased with this new help for the injured, began to call the ambulance regularly. So it was not surprising, on the day when Lee heard a truck rumbling down through the valley, full throttle with its horn blasting, that the minister and his motley crew climbed into the ambulance *before* the accident happened. Lee had driven trucks and heavy equipment while working his way through college and was pretty sure the trucker had lost his brakes. Judging from the sound, the truck was heavily loaded and would never make it past Dead Man's Curve.

A couple of The Bishop's Riders were just closing the hood of the ambulance when the convertible screeched into the church lot. Without waiting for the fire signal, they took off down the hill. They got there just after the trucker had laid his rig over into the side of the hill to stop it. The driver jumped free, the boys stopped traffic, the Highway Patrol arrived, and everybody waited to see whether the rig would explode.

Nothing happened, unless you call the dumping of a refrigerator truckful of frozen chickens over a major highway a happening. Opportunity! There were lots of poor people in our community who could use those chickens. "Help yourself," said the driver. "They're no good to me now." Quicky, Lee and his two helpers began to pack the ambulance full of frozen chickens. From floor to ceiling. With just enough space left for one boy to sit in the back. Talk about manna from heaven!

The ambulance full, Lee closed the back and walked around to the driver's side. There he stood open-mouthed, his hand on the door handle, and watched. Up the hill, in the slowly moving traffic, came a car with a couple so intent on looking at the accident that they drove right off the side of the mountain, crashing and tumbling over the manzanita and rocks. "Get the chickens out. We've got people down there," Lee yelled as he scrambled over the edge after them.

The small crowd that had gathered went into action. The driver was trapped in the car and had to be pried loose; the woman passenger lay off to one side, thrown out of the vehicle. Carefully they were transferred to the waiting stretchers, and with sirens blaring, the crew careened down the mountain.

As soon as the people were safely deposited in the emergency room at the city hospital, Lee and the boys jumped in the ambulance and hurried back to reclaim their chickens before they thawed. The truck was still there, but not a chicken was in sight. All had been claimed by the crowd.

Slightly downcast, the three returned home. They reminded themselves that they had probably saved the lives of two people, even though they hadn't been able to help feed the community. To bolster their spirits, Lee called the hospital to inquire about the patients.

"What's wrong with that ambulance?" the emergency room attendant wanted to know. "Those people had bad cuts and bruises, inside and out, but all they could talk about was how *cold* the ambulance was. Why," he concluded, "their body temperature was so low they darn near had frostbite!"

No need to explain about the chickens. . . .He wouldn't have believed it anyway. . . .

The mountain people laughed for days.


5

Meanwhile, back at the house on the hill, the chilly nights were beginning to take their toll. I was spending more time with my feet up off the cold floor—unless it was night, and then I looked for the warmest body I could find to snuggle against. After all, when we went to bed, so did the heaters.

Lee couldn't be convinced that I was really cold. This was California, the land of perpetual sunshine. He still drove with the top down, except when Mark and I were with him. Every morning there were lizards on the kitchen floor (which he had to dispose of before I would fix breakfast). I argued that they must have come inside to get warm. One morning the kitchen thermometer read 39°, and the canary was frozen solid in its cage. After that, Lee was the first one up. He would jump out of bed, light the heaters, and dive back under the covers before the chill reached him. In my pregnant condition, such agility was impossible.

As the temperature continued to fall I recalled the laughter of our New Jersey friends when our new convertible had been snowed in. Surely it wouldn't happen in California? A parishioner took us up to a higher mountain to show us the remains of an old ski resort that had been forced to close because of the warming climate—a reassuring thought. But when Christmas arrived, the first snow fell. Since December 26 was the date the baby was to be born, I inquired whether the ambulance had snow tires or chains. "Don't need them up here," I was told. "The roads are always clear."

A particularly bad holiday accident sent the ambulance crew out four days after Christmas, and on the return trip the motor began to make an ominous sound. Lee was busy with the church, The Bishop's Riders were occupied with holiday celebrations. So the ambulance sat outside our door with the head off its motor, waiting for parts from town.

The last day of December arrived sunny but cold. Ice patches had been forming on the roads in the mornings, making driving more hazardous than usual. The baby was now six days overdue, so the drive down the mountain was never far from my mind. Lee comforted me: the motor parts would be in day after tomorrow, and with the ambulance in top form, I would coast down the hill on a cloud of ease. I wasn't so sure.

A gala New Year's Eve event was planned at the church. From nine until ten there would be a huge dinner—an organized potluck—and all the families in the community were invited. After dinner, the games and square dancing would begin. At eleven o'clock, the worship service would turn everyone's thoughts to the seriousness of life and the passing of time. Worship would end with Communion just before midnight. Lee had planned a special time in the service for people to write out their resolutions for the coming year. These would be placed on the altar when the people came forward for Communion. At midnight the mood would switch back to partying and well-wishing. No celebration like this had ever been held in the community before.

About three in the afternoon, I decided it would not be wise for me to go. There seemed to be some light twinges going on inside me. When Lee left at seven to get the church ready, I was already deep in an armchair with a good book. Mark was playing with his trucks on the floor, and the two of us settled down for a quiet evening by the unvented heater.

The clock struck eight. Mark and I pretended it was midnight. We blew horns, drank ginger ale, and he went right to sleep at his usual bedtime. By nine, I knew that things were definitely stirring. I watched the clock, remembering that the second baby sometimes comes faster than the first—and that my mother had given birth to one child in the labor room. But I didn't want to ruin the party.

Contractions were coming every five minutes by the time ten o'clock rolled around. The doctor was on the mountain tonight, so I decided to call Lee. If he could take me to her office for a quick check during the games and dancing, he could return to conduct the worship service before it was time to go to the hospital.

Minutes after my call, Lee was home. He brought a sitter with him, and as soon as I was in the car he shot down the driveway as if he were driving the ambulance instead of the convertible. It wasn't until we came to the main highway turnoff that I realized he hadn't heard me. He knew only that the baby was coming, and he was heading for the hospital. He might as well have, since no sooner had the doctor checked me than she sent us on our way, promising to be right behind us.

Lee took off at seventy miles an hour. I offered to drive.

"Don't be ridiculous, Ruth. I just wish I had the ambulance. All the times I've gone down this mountain, and here we are—no sirens, no lights, nothing." I tried to soothe him so he would slow down, but the pains had picked up and it was difficult to talk. I thought about the ice patches, then reminded myself that Lee had lots of experience on this road. We whizzed around Dead Man's Curve. I gave thanks for our safety.

"What about the service?" I gasped between contractions. "Who's going to do it?"

"I don't know. Probably the lay leader will take over." His voice trailed off. Clearly, he had forgotten about the service.

At twenty minutes before twelve we slid to a halt at the emergency room door. By the time I had been wheeled to the maternity floor, my doctor was scrubbing. Lee leaned over and whispered, "If you hurry, we'll have a tax deduction." Of all the nerve! Hurry so we could have a tax deduction? As if I could hurry! I heard nurses talking in the hall. "Do you think we'll have the first baby of the New Year? We've got a chance now!" I felt like the chicken about to lay the golden egg. A nurse gave me a shot, and as I drifted into a dreamy oblivion, I wondered if they did anything special for the first baby of the New Year.

My haze was broken by hands helping me onto the delivery table. Far away, I heard someone say that another hospital had called in to report a child born ten minutes after midnight. "I bet her doctor broke her water just to be first," a voice exclaimed. My bleary eyes searched for a clock. What time was it? Now Lee wouldn't have a tax deduction, and our baby wouldn't be the New Year's Baby. I didn't care. I just wanted it to be whole.

At twenty minutes before one, just one hour after our arrival at the hospital, Becky was born—red-haired, blue-eyed, and whole. She was the first baby born in *that* hospital on New Year's Day. Of course I didn't know that until Lee walked in the next morning with the newspaper. There on the front page were a grinning Lee, the baby, and a *nurse*. The mother? She was mentioned in small print. After all, she wasn't up to having her picture taken!

"What happened last night?" I asked.

"You had a baby, that's what." Lee beamed proudly.

"No, I mean the service. What happened to the service?"

"Oh . . . well . . . it broke up. They all went home."

But they *hadn't* just gone home. In a half dozen houses families had waited in vain for Lee to call them with the news, finally going to bed exhausted about four o'clock. Early that morning the party lines buzzed. We didn't know it then, but we had been accepted. Family members wait up for telephone calls; and we had become part of their family.

They still talk about that New Year's Eve party.
Lee still talks about the broken-down ambulance.
And I still talk about our beautiful red-haired Becky.


## 6

Our first year in California was coming to a close. Lee had fulfilled all his requirements for ordination. But there was one problem—his soul was in conflict. Three years in a student church and one here in the mountains had taken their toll. The future was clear: he would pour out every waking moment for very little reward—either material or psychological. His whole life would be open to criticism from all sides, and in the Methodist tradition, he would have very little to say about where he would serve or where his family would live.

Lee's dad had taught him that if a job is important—*really* important—then you give it everything you have, and in that way you can close the day with a clear conscience. Even if nobody else ever commends your work, *you* will know that you have done your best. It was obvious that not all Lee's colleagues had developed that philosophy. The best ministers worked very hard, but some scarcely worked at all. And this was the *church*. It was supposed to be different from all the other organizations in the world. Yet it was full of ambitious politics—maneuvering for conference offices, for "good" churches. There were even people on the *take* instead of on the *give*. Was this really what he wanted to commit his life to?

And Lee had another offer. When we had arrived in California, a business associate of Lee's father had approached him. For a very reasonable sum, he would sell Lee his business and let us pay the balance out of the next year's profits. It was the 1950s and boom-time in the construction industry, especially in California. Grading contractors had a continual backlog of orders. A hard worker like Lee could make a mint. . . . And now the offer was repeated as Lee approached the final ordination decision. Should he split from the church—or forever silence the large natural streak of ambition for wealth which ran through his very being? Should he—*could* he give his destiny into the hands of strangers who probably would never see him as he saw himself?

The year before our arrival the bishop had told us confidently that he would send Lee where there were lots of people. California was growing. Lee had said he was looking at three possibilities: the mission field, the chaplaincy, and (last) the local church. The bishop had responded with finality. He needed men for his churches; anything else—well, Lee could look elsewhere for conference membership—there were more than enough special appointments in this conference already. So it was plain: if Lee wanted to return to his native state, he must plan on being a local pastor.

Part of Lee's problem was that he had married a Methodist; worse yet, a Methodist minister's daughter! And what with traveling all over California while he was growing up, and following construction jobs, he had ended his teen years in a community church affiliated with the Christian & Missionary Alliance (C&MA) denomination. After high school Lee had entered Bible college and there had pledged himself to the foreign mission field. Upon graduation, he realized he needed more than a Bible certificate to do missionary work, so he had transferred to a school that would give him two years of college credit for his three years of Bible study. That's where I came in. We met the second night of the fall semester and six weeks later had decided we belonged together. After all, I was going to the mission field too. . . .

But when Lee wrote the C&MA mission board to tell them his fiancée was a Methodist and that she wished to retain her church membership, but was perfectly willing to go with him under their auspices. . . . he was dropped from their candidate list in the return letter! It was more than disillusioning. . . .

We looked around for another denomination. We would pick something neutral, a church to which neither of us belonged. One by one we discarded churches and boards because of their beliefs or their ways of dealing with people. And finally we came back to The Methodist Church— together—and as Lee would always say afterward, he became an "adopted" son of John Wesley. But now he was faced with a life commitment. Had he made the right choice? Should he even *be* a minister?

His inadequacies stared at him from the bushes, jumped out from behind the rocks as he walked the graveled roads trying to decide. He had never wanted to preach, to get up in front of people and tell them how to live. He barely knew enough about life and faith to keep himself going, much less a congregation. His skill was not in words, but in his hands. He could take cars apart. He knew how to lay a straight grade. He could work at almost any job and make good money with his physical strength. He understood building. . . . He also loved history, had implanted the Scriptures firmly in his mind, and knew theology and biblical criticism. . . . But he was most comfortable working with his hands. Machines stayed put; people didn't. And besides, both of us had intended to enter mission work. What were we doing in this church in California?

A seminary professor who had blasted away at "the so-called call to work for God" had shaken Lee profoundly. Maybe he'd just been taken in by the C&MA church, where status was to be a *missionary* and everything else was less. But we had tried. We had talked to the Methodist mission board. . . . They were into teachers, doctors, engineers—everything but preachers. They had plenty of those, and the idea was to help people in foreign countries become self-sufficient while presenting the gospel to them. Since ministry was what Lee was trained for, then that's what he ought to do. . . . I had wept long nights, for I was committed equally to husband and to mission, and now my husband was turning away from our original goal. Late one night, his voice hoarse with struggle, Lee suggested that perhaps he never should have married me; he had spoiled my life, my goals. I was stunned. How could he not know that my commitment was to him as well as to God? Somehow God would lead us to the right answer.

And now there was the septic-tank/potato-cellar church in the middle of nowhere, its people hidden away in the folds of the mountains. The bishop had promised to put us where the population was booming. Instead, we were forty miles from the closest Methodist pastor, and worlds apart from mission.

Mission? Certainly we were in a mission field of sorts. . . .
What was mission, anyway, but helping people? Just because
we could speak the language and hadn't crossed the seas, did
that make us any less missionaries? It was all so confusing.

And then there was money. Lee had expected never to earn
much in the mission field—in fact, he knew he would often
have to raise his own support. But here in the "regular"
church he saw his colleagues vying for churches that paid
ever-better salaries. . . . Yet the best was little by business
standards. . . . And he could go into business. He could be
rich. He knew it. He knew how to strike a hard bargain and
walk away with the heaviest pockets. There was a deep streak
of good old American greed roaming around inside him.

The Board of Ministry was waiting for an answer, so
tentatively, Lee told them he would be ordained. . . . In his
soul, he wasn't sure. On Sunday mornings he would look at
the congregation and know he loved them; at home, he would
agonize over every word he had preached. By the next
Saturday he would be almost physically ill, knowing that
tomorrow he must stand before the sacred desk and proclaim
the Word of God. How could he be so brazen? How could he
assume such responsibility?

June and conference time grew closer. Lee talked less about
ordination. I assumed the decision was final. I made a silk
dress and bought a black straw hat with a beautiful flower
perched on one edge. Even Mark and Becky had newly made
outfits. We would leave the children with their grandparents
during conference, and they would all come together to see
Lee ordained. What a special event in our lives this would be! I
was joyful as we set out for Redlands—this year, with room
reservations in hand.

Early on the Sunday of ordination, I woke in the college
dormitory room to find that Lee's bed had not been slept in. I
had left him talking with friends the night before and had
fallen asleep soon after I reached our room. Alarmed, I dressed
quickly and went looking for him. He was in the tiny chapel,
his face contorted with struggle, his tall frame convulsed with
soul-heaving sobs. He had walked and prayed all night, but no
peace had come. Like Jacob he had wrestled with the angel,

but God hadn't struck him with a new identity. He was still Lee Truman—awkward, bumbling, inept. I'd never seen him shake with sobs, never seen him cry . . . except for a single tear that might escape his self-control.

"Is there anyone you can talk to, Lee? How about Ken? Could you talk to him?" Ken was on the Board of Ministry and had been Lee's "big brother" during the year. On his first visit to our borrowed house, Ken had won Lee's heart by arriving in jeans and boots—not at all the suit-and-tie version of minister that now was part of Lee's fear.

With Lee's consent I went looking for our friend. People were coming out of the dining room, and the Board of Ministry was gathering to attend to last-minute details of ordination day. I found Ken, he listened, then went to Lee. I waited.

Nothing Lee told me later made any sense. Ken's words had been no different from those I had used, or words Lee himself had spoken. But somehow Ken's had been right. Lee came forth from his tomb of despair and uncertainty to walk upright in the bright California sunshine. He would be ordained.

Grandparents arrived on schedule with the children. I put on my new silk dress and straw hat. The crowd assembled. Lee stood in line in his handmade pulpit robe with his peers, joking, excited. The procession began and we took our places on the platform, looking into the faces of more than fifteen hundred friends and relatives—almost all of them Methodists. The bishop addressed the men (no women, then) to be ordained. Finally they all knelt, with their wives standing behind them. The bishop's words trembled in the air as his hand came to rest on Lee's head: "Take thou authority to preach the gospel . . ." It was done.

Later that night after the reception and welcoming words from so many people, after our children and their grandparents had gone home, Lee and I held one another, listening to the peaceful night sounds.

"It's not going to be easy, Ruth."

"I know."

"But I'm glad it's done."

"I'm glad too. . . ."

And he slept. The deep, peaceful sleep of a person who has made a good decision and knows it. And like Jacob, he had a new identity. For the first time, he was Lee Truman, ordained Elder of The Methodist Church. He might not be any better preacher, but at least he would preach with authority. The bishop expected him to, and somehow that was nice to know. . . .

7

The congregation grew by six the morning Tiny and his family first visited our church. They were lost Episcopalians living in the mountains with no Episcopal church to meet their needs. Tiny was also an accomplished musician trained in church music, who made his living playing piano in a supper club in the city—which meant that he stayed up very late on Saturday nights. The family liked our basement church and stayed.

Church school classes were enlarged with their arrival, the choir gained a member, and the music changed. When Tiny sat down on the swivel piano stool in front of the old upright, keys came to life that hadn't been touched in years. The choir outperformed itself under his direction, and the congregation literally rose to new heights as he transposed the music of the last verse to a higher key. Sometimes we didn't know whether to sing or just listen, for hymns that had been only precise chords now took on new fills and trills. Church members standing close to the piano often just held their books, watching open-mouthed as Tiny's fingers flew across the keys.

Tiny wasn't his real name of course, but the one he used in his work. It had been given him because of his great size. We all marveled that the piano stool held up under his powerful, energetic style. After all, the stool was as old as the piano.

A summer visitor, hearing this new gift of music in our church, decided she had found the right place for her deceased husband's organ, and soon our new instrument took its place at the right of the pulpit . . . and not a day too soon.

Tiny summoned all his energy one morning to accompany the choir in "The Battle Hymn of the Republic." His head was nodding to keep them on the beat, one foot was working the pedal, the other was counting time, his elbows were flailing, and his fingers were pouncing and dancing on the keys, when with a sudden clatter, the piano stool gave way, collapsing in an irreparable heap. Pieces rolled under the pews and along the altar rail. But only Lee, the choir members, and the front-row sitters knew, for Tiny never missed a beat. Balancing himself in mid-bend, he continued to the end of the number as though nothing had happened. He was a showman—and the show doesn't stop!

Once supplied with an organ, Tiny was there to stay. Any thought of searching for another church was gone—provided some of his demands were met. First, he wanted a screen placed between him and the people. Because of his late night work, he usually arrived on Sunday morning without having had any sleep since Friday. His short naps during the service weren't noticed when he sat on a front pew by the piano—but there was no escape on the organ bench. The screen was there the next Sunday.

The second request was a little harder for Lee to accept. Tiny wanted an electric coffee pot beside the organ. On particularly sleepless weekends, he needed a little caffeine jag to get him through until noon. It wasn't the request that bothered Lee—it was the blurp, blurp, blurp of the perking coffee while he was praying. (Some mornings, Tiny arrived too late to get the coffee started before the service.) And it was the aroma of fresh coffee that wafted through the congregation, making them think it was time for lunch. *And* it was the sight of the organist, sitting behind his rude screen where only Lee and the choir could see him, drinking coffee . . . and nodding his head yes or shaking it *no* as he listened to the sermon! To an Episcopalian, Methodist ideas are not always acceptable!

By the time the organ arrived, Lee had already begun angling for another makeshift carillon (ready-made were too expensive). There was no tower, but Lee hoped the music would make his invisible church visible to the community. All he needed were a turntable, an amp, and a timer in the corner of the tiny office. A seventy-foot pine tree alongside the road nearby served as nature's tower, and with the volume turned high, the music drifted through the valley and slid up the sides of the mountains each evening at dusk.

Someone suggested that they build in an amplifying system for the church at the same time; then it seemed a good idea to tie the new organ into the system so it could be heard either inside or out. We could broadcast some of the magic of Tiny's fingers. As church dismissed and the people exited, Tiny could throw a switch by the organ and the music would follow the people outside and home.

Shortly after the system was in place, one of our members decided he was angry at God. He had lived a good life, honored his debts, provided for his family, and now his wife was dead, his kids never came or called, and his health was beginning to fail. One Sunday he made up his mind he wouldn't go to church—maybe not ever again. So with a gun over one shoulder and his dog by his side, he scrambled over the rocks to a favorite hunting spot, loaded his gun, and sat absolutely still, waiting for some small game to show itself. The dog nuzzled next to him in the morning sun. "You're all I've got," he thought as he stroked the trusting head. And God was supposed to be good! Well, enough was enough. From now on he was going to do it *his* way, which was any way he pleased. And he'd never darken the door of the church again!

Meanwhile, Tiny was settling himself on the organ bench. He checked his coffee pot, drew a little brew to see if the flavor was coming through, pulled out the stops for his prelude, and began to play. Maybe it was because he was tired, or maybe because God wanted it that way, but after the prelude, just to make sure he didn't fall asleep and inadvertently bump the keys during the sermon, Tiny decided to throw the switch. This would keep the music from playing inside. Besides, if he turned the organ off there would be a distracting noise when it was restarted for the final hymn. But Tiny didn't know that not only the organ, but the whole sound system was wired to play outside at the flip of his switch.

Lee began to get signals from the usher that his mike wasn't working, so he turned it up. More signals. Finally the amplifier was set at top volume, but nothing was coming through the speakers in the room. Lee made up for it by speaking louder and louder.

Out on the rock the faint sound of a voice began to rise on the wind. Uneasily, the dog sniffed the air. The voice came again, louder now. It stirred the thoughts of our angry member. Finally, with the last twist of the amplifier knob, the words came pounding across the valley right to the rock where our member sat:—"And God said . . ." He jumped to his feet and, with dog in swift pursuit, half-slid, half-ran down the mountain, the voice following him relentlessly. He tried not to listen. His heart pounded as he raced for his house. Surely the walls would shut out the sound. Slamming the door behind him he leaned against it, panting. Only then did he recognize the speaker's voice. It was the minister—not God. And it was coming from that blasted speaker down the road—not from some mysterious heaven. Still breathing heavily from the exertion, he listened as the organ began the last hymn, then abruptly stopped in mid-note as Tiny realized his mistake and flipped the switch back to the inside position.

All week long in his dreams, the voice spoke as our member relived the trauma of Sunday. By Saturday he had decided to forgive God for taking away his wife and leaving him alone. On Sunday morning he was back in church, having vowed never to stay away again.

As far as the rest of us knew, that was probably the only musical mistake Tiny ever made. And we're still not sure it was a mistake. . . .

## 8

When the red house above us on the mountain was put up for rent, summer had moved into the hot days of September, encouraged by dry winds blowing up from the desert. Lee was tired of bending over all the time in our short dentist's house, and I was not looking forward to another winter of lizards and frozen canaries. So we carried our belongings fifty yards higher, armload by wheelbarrow load. Only this time, the man from the fruit stand and his wife lightened our work . . . faithful friends. The house looked over the whole valley on one side, backed up to the national forest (and all its animals) on the other, and provided a fireplace and *vented* heaters in the bedroom area. Bliss is being warm, even if it means moving three times in two years.

Lee had put extra-heavy springs and oversized tires on the convertible in order to make it over the ruts and rocks in the local driveways. Our beautiful car was aging rapidly. Ten or more teenagers often piled in the back to take a top-down ride to church or to a party. Sometimes there was scarcely room for Mark and Becky and me to squeeze in. The back window had to be replaced for the coming winter—partly because of weathering, partly because so many teenagers had sat on it.

Mark was ready to start kindergarten, and Becky spent her days swimming across the floors in a one-legged crawl. I was looking forward to kindergarten too. At least for part of the day she wouldn't be into her brother's toys. He had come a long way since the first time he held her and then announced, "Can we throw her away now?" In fact, he was now her protector, her big brother.

The new house came with a hill ready-made for digging. Soon Mark had roadways, caves, and tunnels for his small army men, and with his dog Danny faithfully at his side, he spent many busy hours. As soon as he came home at noon, he would switch to play clothes and head for his hill.

Danny assumed that since he was with Mark at home, he should be with him at school, too. After seeing Mark aboard at the end of our lane, the dog would find a way to meet the bus when it arrived at school, no matter how we tried to keep him home. Kindergarten ceremonies were marked with an extra that year: Danny the dog received a certificate for perfect attendance!

Becky began to pull herself up with the help of the kitchen table, soon leaving a row of tiny teeth marks along its edge. She was also showing fine artistic talent, splattering food over her high chair, then turning the not-always-empty dish upside down on her head and grinning through the rivulets of strained peas and carrots that trickled down her pudgy cheeks.

The year and a half had produced a thriving church, advertised by an ambulance that roamed all over the mountain area. As many as one hundred fifty people crowded into the basement on Sunday morning, some driving forty-five miles one way. And Lee had learned a lot about these people. For instance, he learned to be very careful about whose driveway he entered. He had once decided to call on a long-time resident, known for her gossipy cantankerous ways, who had asked to be put on the mailing list of our weekly church paper. Did she recognize the convertible as the preacher's car? We'll never know, for when somebody starts shooting at you from their front porch, good sense says *leave fast!* And Lee did!

Unique, eccentric people were the norm in these mountains. A full-blooded native American was the first person Lee baptized by immersion, and in a hot-springs swimming pool! (Methodists usually are sprinkled!) A retired professor bragged that his ancestors came over on the Mayflower until the Indian reminded him that *his* ancestors had *met* them. One member covered the whole territory selling insurance, but always managed to be back when the church doors opened. Another, angry at the world, reclusive and bitter, gradually began to help around the building. A retired Navy officer came home drunk one night, threatening to kill his whole family, and finally gave his life to Christ. There was no end to uniqueness.

And there were poor people. Lots of them. We were just far enough from the city that bill collectors wouldn't come to harass debtors, the rent was cheap (the housing poor), and the rural atmosphere didn't demand fancy clothes. Whatever you had was O.K. because everyone else was wearing whatever they had. One of our wealthier women made the mistake of asking a welfare mother why she had so many children. Didn't she know what was causing it? The prompt rebuff was squelching: "You rich people have your fun; we poor people have ours." With so many different educational backgrounds, economic levels, and reasons for living in the mountains, all were forced to "just be people"—to accept, forgive, and forget.

But how can you forget coffee offered from a hot water bottle? As a woman poured Lee a cup of rubbery-tasting brew early one morning, she explained that she hated to get out of bed without having a cup of coffee—and she equally disliked getting into a cold bed. The solution was simple: pour boiling coffee into the hotwater bottle and slide it under the covers at bedtime. It keeps your feet warm during the night, and *voila!*—warm (definitely tepid) coffee in the morning to help you face the day. It almost ruined Lee's. . . .

As it turned out, that visit was serendipitous.

Lee wore his hair in a crew cut then. It was easy to care for and easy for me to cut, an important factor since the nearest barber shop was fifteen miles down the mountain and not always open. Actually, I'd been cutting his hair since our starving seminary days. The electric clippers had saved us from bankruptcy many a month. I would put the guide attachment over the blades and slide it across his head. Nothing could have been simpler.

He needed a haircut the day of the big wedding, slated as the society event of the city below. Lee had been asked to perform the ceremony because the foster mother of the groom was the organ benefactress. A chapel in the prominent city park was the site of the service, and all the elite would be present. Lee's nervousness showed as he sat down in our kitchen "barber chair."

"You've got to hold still or you'll have holes in your hair."

He sat almost rigid while I carefully clipped the back and evened the neckline, noting his frequent glances at his watch. "I'm planning to arrive thirty minutes before the wedding, just to be . . .," his words were cut short by silence. The clippers had quit.

"Here, maybe I can fix them. It's probably just hair caught in the teeth." Five minutes later we were both beginning to panic. The back of his hair was fine, but the top looked like a wheat field after the threshing machine had made a first pass. A call to the barber in the town below proved fruitless: no answer. Then Lee remembered—the husband of the hot-water-bottle woman used to be a Navy barber. Two tries at the busy party line convinced Lee to get dressed for the wedding while I kept calling. At last I got through. Yes, he would finish the haircut—but he hadn't cut hair for anybody but his children in a long time.

A quick kiss and Lee was gone, dust swirling behind the convertible as it disappeared down the hill. From our porch I could follow his path around the valley, over the brook, and up the other side.

Navy clippers were out and and waiting. It had been a *very* long time since the man had given a crewcut. He was slow. The corners of the flat top had to be just right. As he finished, Lee looked at his watch. He'd be lucky if he got to the church ten minutes before the wedding.

Minutes later in the town fifteen miles below, a startled motorcycle patrolman saw a yellow blur flash past. By the time he started his cycle, the car was out of sight. Traveling as fast as he dared, he could not overtake it. "There's a yellow convertible headed your way—if he makes it down the mountain." The patrol car at the base of the hills took the radio call and waited.

Lee spun his story to the officer: he was on his way to perform a wedding, his hair clippers had failed, he'd had to find a barber, and—looking at his watch—if he took the back way, out of the traffic, he might still make it on time, but barely.

The officer shook his head. "I've heard some good ones, but yours is one of the best. . . . But what the hell, I bit the dust once too. So I'll let you go. But take it easy, will you? My partner up the mountain still can't believe it!" Lee breathed a prayer of gratitude and took off lickety-split.

When he arrived, there was no place near the chapel to park, so he tossed the keys to the attendant, grabbed his robe and book, and ran to the church. Outside the door he stopped and caught his breath. His watch told him it was exactly time for the wedding to begin. Trying to appear composed and cool, he stepped inside.

No one noticed his arrival. The whole wedding party was in a dither. The *soloist* hadn't arrived. She was the star of the local opera company, and the bride's mother refused to start without her! The organist had been instructed to continue playing. The wedding could wait. Lee introduced himself. The mother smiled, patted his hand, and said it was so nice to know you could always count on the minister to be on time.

Fifteen minutes passed . . . thirty. . . . The mother remained adamant. A call to the soloist produced no answer, so she must be en route. Forty minutes later the star strolled in, startled to find herself the object of concern. The wedding was not to begin for another twenty minutes, according to her appointment book. She must speak to her agent.

She sang. Lee stepped onto the platform. Groom, best man, and ushers took their places—in tuxedos complete with pink bow ties, pink cummerbunds, pink carnations, and pink patent-leather shoes. Bridesmaids began their trek down the aisle, each in pink and carrying pink flowers. The bride came into view, wearing pink-tinged satin, accented by a bouquet of pink and white flowers tied with pink ribbons.

The ceremony proceeded smoothly—as if nothing had happened. It began exactly an hour late, but no one seemed to care, as they moved on to the sumptuous reception. Pink champagne flowed, pink wedding cake was dispensed, guests were given pink rice wrapped in pink netting, and the bride and groom left the chapel in a wedding gift—a brand new pink Cadillac!

That's how Lee learned not to think more highly of himself than he should. Maybe it's natural, but to this day when he talks about that wedding, he laughs until his cheeks turn . . . what else? . . . pink!

9

Our appointment to the mountains also marked the separation of another congregation—a tiny one—from what had been a two-point circuit. No pastor was assigned there, so whenever they needed one they just naturally called Lee. It was on one of those jaunts across the mountains (often through snow and ice) that he found the prison camp. Isolated from most resources for mental and spiritual rehabilitation, the prisoners and warden were delighted with Lee's offer to lead them in experimental sharing groups which combined the spiritual with the psychological. Every week, through fog, snow, ice, and rain, the convertible would disappear down the hill, leaving me to increase my prayer life while pleading for my husband's safe return.

The added income was great—$7.50 a visit! (When you make $387 a month, $7.50 is a whole lot!) More important were the new people who began to drive to our church, people who worked at the prison. Parolled convicts also began to arrive at our doorstep for a night's rest or a meal before going on down into the city to resume their lives. They knew a host of (illegal) tricks which made them extremely entertaining conversationalists. And if they happened to stop on a weekend, they went to church with us, where they worshiped elbow to elbow with the warden. The prison ministry was certainly enlarging our church . . . and Lee's workload.

During this second fall, each of us had a project. Mine was simple: I would entertain the women's society so they could see our new house. Lee had decided the church should respond to the conference call for sponsors to help resettle people from Indonesian World War II refugee camps who were inundating Holland. All I had to do was bake and clean; Lee had to find a house, a job for the family head, and incidentally convince the church that it was a great idea.

For days I scrubbed and baked. Windows were washed, curtains hung, all the furnishings put in place. When the day arrived, I was ready. Women began to arrive, exclaiming over the difficulty of getting their cars up the hill, the view we had, the size of the fireplace. I filled plates with food, poured coffee and tea, and tried to make everyone feel welcome. At my invitation, they were wandering through the house, inspecting our new quarters. A woman approached me with a distressed look. "Have you been in the bathroom lately?"

Red flags went up in my brain. "No, why?"

"I think you ought to take a look." . . . She followed me into the bathroom everyone had been inspecting. Sitting in the middle of the floor was Becky's stepstool; beside it, an empty lipstick container. On the tub, sink, walls, even in the grooves of the switchplate, was flaming red lipstick. Becky's art career had begun. So had days of scrubbing. . . .

Lee's reaction was saner than mine. He laughed, kissed his "princess," and started talking about the refugee family—a couple and their daughter. He was an architect, she a Bali dancer. The letter he thrust into my hand was full of excitement at finally realizing their dream of coming to America.

The whole church caught Lee's enthusiasm and a rental house and an architectural job quickly became available. Letters flew between countries. A welcoming party was planned and several families were going to the city to meet the refugees at the airport.

On the day of arrival Lee and his secretary climbed into her station wagon. She was dressed as usual for work—a plain cotton dress, well-worn flat shoes, an old sweater—whose elbows had long since disappeared. She laughed about her appearance, and Lee said it was fine. It would keep the refugees from feeling uncomfortable in their old clothes.

About thirty hillfolk gathered at the airport. Excitement rose as the plane landed. Passengers began to disembark, but no refugees emerged—only well-dressed tourists and businessmen. Lee looked at the letter. The date was right, the flight number correct. Perhaps he should check the passenger list.

Our group watched as he spoke to the man at the gate, saw the relieved look come across the attendant's face as he pointed to one side. There stood an elegant couple with a small daughter. The woman was wrapped in fur, jewels hung from her ears, her stylish dress was perfectly coordinated with spike-heeled shoes. The man wore an expertly cut suit, white shirt, tie, and expensive leather shoes. The daughter could have modeled for any magazine.

The church people began to move uneasily as understanding dawned. Their minister, clad in blue jeans, sport shirt, and engineer's boots, was shaking hands with the elegant gentleman. Lee beckoned to his secretary. Now it was the "refugee" family's turn to adjust their expectations. "Your *secretary?*"the accented voice inquired. Worn sweater stood face to face with elegant fur. A plain, hard-working hand engulfed the small bejeweled one.

"Welcome to California. . . ."

"Ah, California! It is the Riviera of America, no?"

Actually, no. Wyatt Earp probably never visited the "Riviera," nor had any of our people. But they knew how to welcome newcomers. The shock past, they crowded around our refugees, filled their cars with luggage to begin the caravan through city, past suburbs, up mountains covered with sagebrush and mesquite, through the last small town, finally parking before a humble summer cabin. The refrigerator was full; a steaming supper soon arrived. Beds were waiting with clean sheets and blankets. An old car had materialized to provide transportation to work, but there was a place in a carpool while our family was becoming accustomed to driving in the California mountains.

By February our refugees were grateful. Adjustment to new ideas takes time, you know, and they had been subjected to more new ideas than most. They approached Lee with an idea of their own. To show their appreciation to the community, they would put on a show. The husband was a hypnotist, the wife an expert Balinese dancer (as opposed to "belly" dancer!). Lee gulped and plunged into making arrangements.

The night of the show was fiercely cold, but the hall we had rented was full of warm bodies. Under the hypnotist's skill, people became stiff as boards and others stood on them. There were the usual kind of silly acts designed to titillate the audience. Then our dancer appeared in a costume so scant as to make the holes in the church secretary's sweater seem absolutely opaque. I squirmed. This was a *church* program, after all! What would the people think? But they seemed to be thoroughly enjoying it, albeit some may have been slightly envious—or covetous—of the beautiful figure that gyrated and glided before them.

The concluding act left us speechless. At a command from her husband, our refugee dancer slumped into a trance. Next, to our horror, small pieces of broken soft-drink bottles were scattered on the stage; the dancer obediently lay down on them. Volunteers were asked to inspect the glass shards and then step on a board placed across the dancer's body. Several gingerly did so. Directing his wife to stand, the husband proceeded to pick the pieces of imbedded glass out of her back. Not a drop of blood flowed. The audience was deathly still. Finally the last sliver was removed. The skin closed as if nothing had entered it. Our hypnotist snapped his fingers and his wife stirred slightly, hazily opened her eyes, and, at last reoriented to her surroundings, took a bow.

The house shook with applause. Lee glanced at me and grinned. Not only had it been good entertainment, but the ticket sales were high. The refugees had come through beyond our expectations. By midnight we had cleaned the hall and Lee had already proposed another show. This time we would take it to the city, rent a large hall in a major church. There would be flyers to all the Methodist churches, ads in the papers. An act like this could not only pay back the funds the church had spent to settle the family, but might help the struggling budget as well. His mind leaped with possibilities on the way home.

Our refugee couple agreed. In fact, they were pleased at the prospect of performing in the city. They probably hoped it would afford them a ticket to Hollywood, an escape from the mountains. Gleams of the warm "Riviera" country fairly flashed in their eyes. Lee secured the hall, the advertising went out, and the big night arrived.

The hall seated five hundred. Fifteen minutes before performance time three people were present, besides the church committee, Lee, and me. Then the district superintendent arrived with his wife. No one else came.

We waited five minutes, ten, fifteen. Backstage, Lee suggested they give the show anyway—at least part of it. The dancer refused. She would be insulted to perform before so few people! Her voice could be heard distinctly in the hall. At last she was persuaded to "demonstrate" her dancing. Lee mumbled some words of apology and offered refunds to the five paying customers. Fortunately they refused, since our budget had been demolished by renting the hall and lights. The evening was a disaster.

Furthermore, some people had never recovered from the first show. Weeks afterward, Lee was hailed by a parishioner. Did he know "that woman" was sitting outside in her shorts and bra? Lee was confused. The refugee family's house was on the opposite side of the valley.

"Look for yourself," said our parishioner, handing Lee a pair of heavy binoculars. He looked. There in her own backyard, enjoying the first warm sun of spring, sat our dancer in shorts and bra. She appeared to be sewing sequins onto a costume. Suddenly Lee felt foolish, tricked into spying. Without a word he handed back the glasses and climbed into the car. After all, what was there to say?

He had learned a lot about Bali dancing, and about how one parishioner kept tabs on everything that went on in the valley. And not for fifteen years would he have enough nerve to sponsor another refugee family.


## 10

While Lee was wrestling with his refugees, I had a new problem. Actually, *we* did. We were pregnant again.

It seemed like a good idea at the time to have two children close together so they could grow up as playmates and friends. We estimated seventeen months apart to be just about right. There was one basic question we forgot to ask: right for whom? My body was the first to complain. I had recently been through this same trauma and now screamed for extra B vitamins. With medical care so far removed, the morning ritual soon included plunging a hypodermic needle filled with B-complex deep into my upper leg. It was simple after I learned how: just raise the needle into position over the trembling leg, close my eyes, grit my teeth, and plunge away before I could realize what was happening. . . .

The schedule also plunged fearlessly forward. Meetings, dinners, entertaining, hurried trips to the city, diapers, cleaning, choir. We both ran faster to keep up, but it was never fast enough. As the echoes of the Bali dancing fiasco faded into new spring leaves, we found ourselves exhausted at the end of each day but trusting the fact that—after all—we were *very* young. Vacation time would soon be here.

Five weeks before the baby was to be born, my sleep was interrupted one morning by the bed. It was shaking violently. "Oh God, not an earthquake—not now, not when I can scarcely move," I prayed. The bed kept shaking. I looked around the room. Nothing else was moving—not the overhead light, not the pictures, not the tables. As all heavily pregnant women do, I rolled over to a sitting position, fully awake. The bed was shaking because Lee was shaking! He was curled into a ball; his teeth were chattering.

Haltingly, he apologized for waking me. "Call the doctor, will you?" The words followed me into the living room on my way to the phone.

"Your call doesn't surprise me, Ruth," came the familiar voice of our doctor, who a year earlier had refused to recommend Lee for the ministry unless she could specify that he must take frequent vacations. "Lee is probably in the midst of a full-blown nervous breakdown." She would come immediately.

Meantime, what was I to do? Sunday was two days away. Somebody had to preach. A moan came through the bedroom door. Lee didn't seem the breakdown type to me, but I didn't even know how a person with a breakdown looked.

And it was almost time to wake Mark for school, and that meant Becky would be awake to be changed and bathed. Without hesitation, I did what every intelligent young woman does: I called my mother. My beautiful blessed mother, who could preach and pray just as easily as she could rock a baby to sleep.

While Mother was buying her plane ticket in Michigan, we were hurrying Lee down the hill to the hospital. To my great relief, his fever had shot up by the time the doctor arrived. Infection is a lot easier to treat than mental collapse! A new word was added to our vocabulary—pyelonephritis (a kidney disease).

Mother emerged from the plane green with nausea and migraine. The "red-eye special" had connected that morning with a commuter plane full of cigar smoke. That, coupled with lack of sleep, had presented her with a violent case of motion sickness. But twenty-four hours later when she stood in the pulpit, no one could tell. (And under the circumstances, it never occurred to anyone to question the authority of a *woman* preacher!)

By midweek Lee was responding to treatment and agitating to come home. A major part of his recovery program was flat-in-bed rest. I was becoming more exhausted, traveling back and forth to the city, so on the basis of his promise to stay down, the doctor scheduled his release for Thursday. Good news! I started back up the mountain on Wednesday afternoon, glad that this was the next-to-last trip. At home, I stretched my heavy body out on the bed for a quick nap before relieving Mother of the children. She was beginning to wilt a little, too.

Twenty minutes later a familiar pain ran through my back, bringing me totally alert. It couldn't be. Lying perfectly still, I waited. Five minutes went by. It came again. Another five minutes. Again. . . .

A neighbor came to stay with the children and down the hill we went, Mother and I, with labor contractions moving steadily closer together. Had we figured the time wrong? It was still a month until time for the child to be born.

I walked into the labor room under my own power, surprised to find a friend from our community in the other bed. We would have a race to see which one gave birth first—and we'd share a room afterward.

Comfortably settled, the time between my pains suddenly decreased to seven minutes, then ten. I walked the halls. They moved up to five, then became erratic. I was too tense, they said. All night I walked, rested, walked, while Mother waited. By morning a specialist was called in. He decided it was just false labor. Morphine would relax me and the pains would stop. Home on the mountain, I slept until the morphine wore off. Then everything started again. "Bring her back," was the instruction.

The next hours faded out. It was real labor. My body was simply too tired to help the child. Soon fluids were dripping into my arm. From somewhere, Lee appeared (later I would learn that when he was dismissed from the hospital, he had come straight to my room). I heard the word *Caesarean* spoken in the hall, and my body drew upon a last ounce of determined strength. Minutes later the baby was born.

I opened my eyes in the delivery room. The incubator was empty. "Where is he?"

"They've taken him to the nursery where they can care for him better." I drifted off. Lee's face appeared above me with a reassuring smile, then he was gone. My intended roommate had already left the hospital. Two nights and most of three days had passed since that first quiet pain had wakened me.

Saturday feeding time arrived, but my baby didn't. Other babies were brought to mothers for nursing, but not mine. Finally I asked about my baby. "Didn't the doctor tell you?" was the nurse's response. Tell me what? I would have to wait until he came in the morning, but if I would like to walk down to the nursery, I could see my baby.

He was black and blue. His breath came in uncertain gasps, stopped altogether, then started again. Each time, his chest sank while his belly seemed to swell with air. The nurse gently pried me from the window and I went back to my room to pray.

Sunday dawned. The doctor told me our child might not make it. They would have to keep him in the hospital in an isolette until the fluid was out of his lungs. He might have a hernia in his diaphragm. It was too soon to tell what the permanent effects might be, but if he lived, he would at least have respiratory troubles.

I began to pray for Timothy. Timothy Wallace. Since Mark shared one of Lee's names, this son should share the other. As I prayed, I watched the clock move toward the hour for church. Mother would be preaching again. God . . . O God, let Timothy live and be whole. . . .

In the basement church our people were gathering for worship. As was their custom, two small candles were lighted in honor of the two new lives. My friend had delivered a healthy girl, so there was a candle for her; and there was one for Timmy. Carefully the acolyte touched the flame to each wick and the service began. Hymns were sung, prayers offered—among them, prayers for Timothy. Mother began to preach. From somewhere a breeze swept toward the altar and one of the small flames began to flicker. The congregation held its breath as a choir member moved over to protect the flame with his hand. The preaching stopped. Everyone prayed silently, watching the flame shrink. Determined, the man shielded the flame with both hands, trying to find the source of the draft. No one moved. At last, slowly, the flame rose, gaining strength till it burned tall and bright again. Mother prayed. People wept.

In the hospital, my soul was suddenly stilled. Tim would live. I knew it. God had heard my prayer. Giving praise I slipped serenely into a morning nap. All I had to do now was put his name on the birth certificate. . . .

"Call him what? *Luke Arn*? Where did you get that?" Against doctor's orders, Lee had come to take me home, but first we must sign the birth certificate. "We already have Mark. If we name him Luke, everybody will always want to know where Matthew and John are." Lee was fighting a losing battle this time. He laid out his arguments to no avail. After all, our child was making rapid improvement in the nursery, and *God* knew him only by *Timothy*. . . .

Two days later Mother and I went down the hill one more time, leaving Lee stretched out on the couch watching Becky. Tim was five days old and the hospital was pleased to tell us we could take him home! Joyfully we took turns holding the precious bundle. His breathing was even, and he was eating—had in fact gained weight. Right now it didn't matter that there were three children and a sick husband to care for. Lee would get better. Mother would stay another week. By then I would be rested and ready to take over again. As we turned up the lane, the house on top of the hill was a welcome sight. We would put the baby to bed and all take a rest.

We stepped in the back door. Lee was sound asleep on the couch. Becky sat in the middle of the kitchen floor, her head, face, and hands covered with lard and flour. Then we saw: the same mixture was artfully spread across kitchen cabinets, windows, dining table, floor. Eyes sparkling, red curls bouncing, Becky toddled toward us with outstretched arms. There was nothing to do but hug her and clean her up.

And Lee? Well, he was sick, so who could blame him for going to sleep?

Order restored, we laughed over coffee. Nothing could dismay us right now. Lee was getting well. Our child had lived. Our two other children were growing, healthy and creative (that's what we called the lard and flour project). And Mother's strength was strength to us.

The next evening the phone rang. It was my minister father, slightly frantic. Could Mother come home right away? Conference was in session, and he had just been told they were going to move.

She stayed to preach one more time before boarding the train for Michigan. It was cheaper to go back by train, she said, and besides, the memory of motion sickness was very strong. Years later, she would confess the real reason for going home by train: two-and-a-half lovely days of solitude and rest before packing. She was simply exhausted. . . .

It must have been catching!


## 11

With Mother gone, Lee and I sat down to assess our situation. No doubt about it. Our two years in the mountains had been hectic. It wasn't just the increase in the family or the schedule at the church. Life at the top of the hill was a full adventure in itself because of all the others who lived with us.

Wild howls in the night signaled coyotes or mountain lions prowling above in their constant search for food. And while those screams sent chills down my spine when I was home alone with the children (shades of the cat down the well!), there was also a continual array of smaller animals to deal with.

The fall before Tim was born, a stray cat had presented Mark with four kittens, duly dubbed Muff, Puff, Fluff, and Scuff. Those were their *Christian* names. Through the open back door soon after their birth, I heard our son's small voice: "I baptize thee in the name of the Father, the Son, and the Holy Spirit." Tiptoeing to the window, I saw each kitten splashed with water and then replaced beside the mother cat.

As the kittens began to grow, the garbage-disposal team appeared. At eight o'clock almost every winter evening, the clatter of the garbage-can lid signaled their arrival, and we would gather to watch as two masked raccoon, one on each side of the can, lifted the lid. Though we never saw it happen, we suspected they also accounted for the disappearance of all but one kitten.

The weather became colder, and we hosted a family of skunks exactly under the floor of our bedroom closet. They had to be smoked out, and there went a pair of Lee's jeans and a T-shirt, with no money to replace them. Skunks can sure spray a long way. . . .

The winter cold also brought freezing temperatures to our unheated living-room/kitchen area, so that any foray into that part of the house at night when a child was sick was a frigid experience—to say nothing of preparing breakfast in a 40° room while Lee fanned the fire with numb hands. Maybe we ought to have a talk with our district superintendent. Maybe—just maybe—we needed to move.

He was polite, encouraging, and final. There was nothing open for us that year. We had come too late. Besides, we were doing such a *good* job in the mountains.

I cried all the way back up the hill. It wasn't that I didn't love the people or the church. I was just so tired of fighting the elements. And now with a new baby. . . . Lee patted my hand. We'd make it all right. Maybe we could get another heater for the living room.

"O.K.," I announced through my runny nose. "But if we're going back for another year, we're going to buy a parsonage!" Lee spent the rest of the trip telling me why we couldn't do that. I never heard a word he said.

Through the summer we nursed Tim's fragile life. Anyone else would catch a cold, but Tim would have bronchial pneumonia. Wheezing in the night brought us to our feet. The pediatrician who had attended his birth reminded us that he had warned of such things. Time was proving him right as Tim was diagnosed as "allergic to infection," and monthly trips down the hill for gamma globulin shots depleted our already stretched income even further.

Lee and I spent more time apart—while he attended church meetings and functions, I was home with the children. There were no neighbors, and as meetings ran later and later, I would feel the old tide of fear rising inside me. Mark had to be in bed early in order to be up for school, Becky soon followed, and I would be left alone with Tim.

With two children already occupying the second bedroom, the large laundry area was the only place to put Tim's crib and chest so that the other children would not be disturbed when he cried during the night. On long lonely evenings when Mark and Becky were in bed, I would rock him until he relaxed into deep sleep, then ever so gently lay him in his crib.

One hot dark night, the raccoon made more noise then usual. They wanted the baby rabbit the cat had caught, and when I opened the door, she was more than glad to drop the rabbit and dash to safety. With that crisis past, I sat holding a wheezing Tim in my lap, Mark and Becky snuggled on either side to hear their favorite stories. At last they were tucked in bed and asleep. Only Tim's labored breathing broke the silence. My own weariness was adding to the tenseness of the late hour, so I carefully shifted to my feet and walked silently to his crib. Dressed only in a shirt and diaper, he squirmed about until his tiny body was comfortable.

Ever fearful of drafts that would increase his bronchitis, I picked up a receiving blanket that lay at the end of the crib and, with horror, watched as a scorpion, its stinger twitching, fell from the folds of the blanket onto Tim's back. Slowly it began to walk toward his bare neck, tail poised to strike. Grabbing the thick pad of tissues I kept on the bed, I clutched at the tiny monster. Pulling back, I gasped to see that not only had I missed it, but now it was angry. I tried again, this time making sure the scorpion was in my grasp. Dropping the tissues to the floor, I stamped on them over and over again. At last, sure that the scorpion was dead and there were no others, I slumped against the wall, completely unnerved.

At that moment I heard our car coming up the hill. Lee was finally home! By the time he walked in, I was sobbing.

"Look what almost killed our baby!" He picked up the scorpion remains. "We've got to have a house, Lee. A *real* house."

"Maybe there is one, Ruth," he murmured as he held me against his big comforting shoulder. "Maybe the house with the lawn will be for sale soon." It was the *only* house in the community with a lawn *and* a full heating system at a price the church might be able to afford. Even through my tears, I began to thank God for scorpions. We had already given thanks for saving our son. . . .

Fall turned into winter. The snow was so deep we couldn't get the car up the hill, but the youth group had a great time tobogganing down the road. Tim's colds increased. Twice we rushed him down the mountain to the hospital, his lungs filled with congestion. And twice Lee was again forced to bed with kidney attacks. Still no house came on the market. But the time was not lost. The church people were getting used to the idea that they needed to buy a house. They talked to one another until it became common knowledge that they were *going* to purchase a parsonage just as soon as the right one was available. They even talked about building one.

But no one knew where to find the money. City banks wouldn't loan us any because we were outside the water district. Not enough was available through the national church mission board. Pledges barely covered the outstanding loans on the property and church basement building. People were already giving all they could.

Spring brought a For Sale sign on the house with the lawn. Lee was back in the hospital with a fourth (and final!) kidney attack and the doctors were telling him to slow down or be dead before he was forty. This time there was no mother to call; she was busy putting her new life together. I was the one who had to preach and pray—and hold administrative board meetings (we called it official board then). When the church resolved to buy the house if we could get a loan, I decided there was just one person to call: the lady of the organ and pink-wedding fame. If she could give away an organ and a Cadillac, I was sure she had enough money to finance our loan. From his sickbed Lee gave me permission to put through the call. The next day her business manager was there to look at the house. We had our loan!

We still had to have conference permission, however. The church committee and I met with the district building committee. They asked questions we didn't have answers for. How far apart were the supporting beams? What kind of foundation did it have? Our replies were sketchy at best. Finally we simply pleaded that this was the best house in the community—a community which none of them except the D.S. had ever seen—and that if they'd like to drive up the mountain, we'd be glad to show them the wisdom of our choice.

The D.S. intervened. "If the church committee thinks this is the best house up there, we can dispense with all these questions. There aren't too many permanent houses for them to choose from." And turning to us, "You're lucky to find a good house. Does it have an adequate *heating* system?"

Bless him. He must have known I couldn't make it through another winter just *pretending* it never gets cold in California. Lee might accomplish that, but we Michiganders recognize snow and ice when we see it.


12


The next few weeks were full of feverish activity. Lee was back at work, overseeing the papers on the purchase. The women's society president and I studied the house to make a work plan, and a date was set for a consecration service.

Palm Sunday was chosen as the day. The D.S. and his wife would come, and he would lead a service of ritual and prayers on the lawn. A Methodist Parsonage sign would be hung on the new lamppost by the walk. Of course there would be refreshments for the people as they toured the house and grounds.

Scrubbing and painting filled our days. We began to move our belongings, a carload at a time (better than a wheelbarrow!), until the house on the hill was half bare and the new parsonage half full. The beds were to be moved on the

Saturday before Palm Sunday, and we would sleep in the new house that night.

On Thursday Becky began to run a fever. Twenty-four hours later, it was obvious: she had the old-fashioned measles. We couldn't move her to the new house until all the people had left. A string of people took turns watching Becky while we dashed back and forth.

Mid-afternoon on Saturday, the women and I were hanging the last drapery in the living room when the phone rang. I listened, turned to the women's president and asked, "What's a quick way to sober somebody up?" She never stopped hanging the draperies. "Beats me." My poor caller was in a pickle. She had spent all her grocery money on beer, was now quite drunk—as well as quite pregnant—and feared her husband would be very angry if she wasn't sober when he came home from work.

"There's only one thing I know to do," I began. (There really was only one thing I knew, and I was making it up right then!) "Your baby needs oxygen and you need sobering up, so make yourself a full pot of strong coffee, go out on the back step with it, and breathe deep and drink it all." I hung up the phone and turned to see my helper covering her mouth to keep from laughing. "She's gonna hate you! She'll be *so* sick!"

That night Mark, Tim, and I slept in the new house and Lee spent the night on the couch in the house on the hill. Becky was now completely covered with angry red blotches, but the fever was gone, and she was delighted to have her daddy all to herself.

Next day even the weather celebrated. Everyone who had ever come to church was there—even my caller of the previous day, who informed me she had sobered up all right, but not until she had lost an entire day's supply of food and alcohol! But never mind. The sign was hung, the prayers prayed. Cookies disappeared. Church members said how relieved they were to have a home for their minister; no more renting.

And finally it was over. The sun was sliding behind the mountains when Lee claimed our mottled two-and-a-half-year-old daughter from the house on the hill. Mark busied himself opening every drawer, exploring the yard and garage. In this new world there were also playmates from school just across the road! And Lee and I counted the kitchen cabinets—all twenty-seven of them. He explained the fireplace supplemental heating arrangement, but assured me that it was in addition to the forced-air furnace. For the first time in three years, we lay our heads on pillows in a house with insulation and heat. No more scorpions, no more freezing breakfasts, no more isolation—there were neighbors all around. We'd never forget this Palm Sunday!

While we were making changes it seemed a good time to change automobiles too. Our beautiful yellow convertible just wasn't any more. It had been thrashed by weather, rough roads, and teenagers. Besides, it was time for the station wagon our growing family needed. Sadly we parted with the car from the New Jersey showroom floor; a white station wagon took its place in the garage.

In June, Lee and I went to Redlands for Annual Conference. There was no need to ask for a change of churches this year, for we had solved the housing problem and had lots to do in this community. Two days before the end of the conference, we were standing in line at the commissary. The man ahead of us turned to look at Lee's name tag. "Lee Truman! You're the guy who's going to follow me!" Bewildered, we looked at each other—then at *his* name tag. Where was he from? Neither of us recognized the name of the town.

We bolted from the lunchroom and went looking for the D.S. Was this rumor or truth? Why hadn't we been told? Was that the only place we could move? Were they certain we *should* move? Why? Could we look at our options?

A quick trip into Los Angeles, then another conference with the D.S. The lay delegate from our mountain church—the man who had protected the flame on Tim's candle—heard we were to be moved and the next day was hospitalized, suddenly old and ill. The conference cabinet made a decision, and on Sunday we heard our name read. We were assigned to a place perfect for a convertible . . . now that ours was gone.

Lee spent the next week calling on people to explain the mysteries of the appointment system. Between visits, he collected boxes from behind Perkins' Store. It was quickly evident that the supply would have to be enlarged . . . so he decided to visit a trucker's station and perhaps gather a few more cartons. The owner was in his house up on the hill. A lot had happened to that man during our three years. His family had broken up, his wife and children moved away. . . . Lee knocked on the door.

"Come in," called a slurred voice. Lee pushed open the unpainted door and found himself facing a gun barrel. He did not doubt that the weapon was loaded. Carefully, talking all the time, he edged into a chair opposite our friend. As if the gun did not exist, Lee began to talk about the good times they had experienced together; he explained why we were leaving. The gun never moved, and its owner's drunken answers did not mention the weapon.

Finally Lee rose to leave, the gun barrel following him upward, staying perilously in line with his heart. As cautiously as he had entered, he closed the door and directed his steps calmly back to the car, waiting for a shot to ring out. Nothing happened. He climbed into the driver's seat and was halfway home before he remembered the boxes. Somehow they didn't seem very important—not enough to go back! For years he would wonder why our friend held the gun on him the whole time they visited—or why at all? He was just grateful to reach home alive that day. . . .

Boxes continued to pile up in the garage, the living room, our beautiful twenty-seven cupboard kitchen. Just ten weeks after we had moved into our parsonage, we loaded all our belongings—for the fifth time in three years! We kissed our people, hugged, cried. Three of us had come, five were leaving. The dog stayed behind on a ranch, to live out his days in the freedom to which he was accustomed.

Miles faded the memories as we resolutely set our faces toward the new appointment. Countryside disappeared even as blue sky faded into brown smog. Freeways joined freeways until we finally turned off to make our way through an industrial section, past railroad yards to the traffic signal where we would turn left. One block from that corner was our new church. That's when it hit me.

"Lee, do you remember last year when we came up here and you spoke at that district youth rally? We passed a corner and I said I'd sure never want to live there?"

Lee nodded assent.

"Lee . . . this is the corner." By the time I had finished the sentence he was pulling into the parking lot beside our new home.

# The Middle, Second Half

How long, O Lord, how long?

## 1

We stepped inside the front door and breathed a sigh of relief! There was furniture!—and a carpet! At conference the D.S. had told us we would need to meet with the church committee to discuss furnishing the house, because the minister who had preceded us had owned all the furniture and now there was none. Last church, no house. This church, no furniture!

We had made a hurried trip to the local stores with the committee and helped choose a couch and dining-room set. With a couple of end tables and the things we had, the house would be fairly well furnished. But from the minute we had begun to look at carpet, I knew I was in trouble—again. The chairperson obviously had the most clout, and he wanted the same kind of carpet in the parsonage that he had in his beautiful large house on the hill: light—almost white—beige. I didn't know these people; they didn't know me. How much did I dare say?

"Children might be hard on such a rug—it might be difficult to keep clean . . . ," my fears were hidden behind calm words of quiet protest. Other committee members agreed, but there was only one couch that seemed to fit the room—one in *that* store, that is—and in the price range the church could afford. It was black. Obviously the pale rug looked best with the black couch. And it was just as apparent that the committee didn't plan to spend more time shopping around.

"We've had ours for two years and it looks like new," replied the chairman. "We just take our shoes off at the front door." I tried to imagine asking the women's society president to take her shoes off, or a route through the kitchen that the children could take without stepping on the rug. Impossible! The living room flowed directly into the dining room; a short hall led to bedrooms and bath, and all opened onto the carpeted area. Even the kitchen adjoined the carpet-covered dining room. More discussion ensued, but finally I demurred. It wasn't worth alienating people or ruining Lee's welcome into this church. I would do my best with an almost-white rug.

Now as we entered the house, it indeed looked lovely. The end tables were topped with modest lamps, the dining set was in place under a new light fixture, and we felt welcomed. We needed that welcome. We hadn't finished packing the moving van until 12:45 A.M. this very day. The new bed in the master bedroom looked most inviting, even though it was just off the living room in plain view, in a room originally intended as a pastor's study. Thank heavens for sliding doors!

But there was no time for rest. We needed to plan the placement of our belongings and boxes before the moving van arrived.

Walking gingerly on the new carpet (with our shoes on) we sized up the storage. Closets—make that clo*set*—existed only in the master bedroom. We'd have to put a wardrobe in the kids' room-and-a-half. Bunk beds and the crib would go in the larger room for the boys, and Becky could use the tiny back room. A built-in china closet graced one dining-room wall for the good dishes and wedding-gift silver. With the linen cupboard and a couple of chests, plus the window-seat storage in the dining room, we'd have enough space . . . *inside* the house.

Then we stepped into the kitchen. Lee immediately discovered that he could touch each wall if he stood exactly in the middle of the room. That meant every meal would have to be eaten over the white rug in the dining room—at least every family meal—with Tim in his high chair, Becky knocking over her milk, and Mark trying to help wait on the table, with sometimes disastrous results. But there was hope. Maybe a wall could be knocked out between the kitchen and service porch. . . .

And that ended the tour. No garage. No basement. No attic. Our backyard was the church's side yard. The house was *between* the parking lot and the church. We were soon to discover the "convenience" of that arrangement. It was not church/parking lot/house, nor parking lot/church/house, but parking lot/house/church. As if to emphasize that realization, we simultaneously saw and heard a car pull into the parking lot. A heavyset man got out, came up on the front porch, and pounded on the door.

Not waiting for a response, he called through the screen, "Hi. I'm the treasurer. Just came by to find out how you want your check. If we have any money, it will always be on time," he chuckled. "Of course, we don't always have the money!" Standing on the new rug (with his shoes on), he boomed, "Looks good in here. May not have enough left over to pay the moving van, though. When's it coming?"

We told him the van should arrive any time. His statement had alarmed me, since I knew *we* didn't have money to pay the moving bill. Our visitor disappeared down the hall, looking into every space, his comments drifting behind him. Satisfied that the house had been sufficiently cleaned, he returned to the dining area. "I hear you've got some kids. Where are they? Last preacher's kids burned down the church on Thanksgiving Day. Sure hope yours don't do that!" This time he laughed uproariously. I smiled weakly, glad we had left the children with Lee's parents while we were moving in. People could inspect the house and look us over, but they'd better not malign our children!

With a promise to be back later when the van arrived, our visitor talked himself all the way to his car. Lee followed him out. Inside the house I never missed a word, since there was only a narrow sidewalk between house and parking lot.

Our visitor gone, Lee and I went next door to the church. We had seen the outside on our first quick trip, but had only glanced at the inside the day we'd picked out the furniture. Now we could really look.

When we stepped into the quiet sanctuary, the busy street seemed far away. Sun shone through the slender arched stained-glass windows, casting a spectrum of colors across oak pews and furnishings. It was worshipful and lovely, even with the worn carpets—quite a change from our basement church in the mountains. No pews were movable; nothing was makeshift. I wondered if this was an index to the people. Were they immovable too? But the fine kitchen and social hall off the rear of the sanctuary whisked my thought away. Everything on this level was just ten years old, and as we went down to the basement classrooms, I was thinking that the preacher's kids had probably done the church a favor! The congregation had produced a beautiful building from the flames. After all, God *does* work in mysterious ways. . . .

Lee discovered a small but shelf-lined study for the pastor, so when the van finally arrived at 5:15 P.M. he was ready to get his books out and start to work. Unfortunately, the driver of the van wasn't. He had no helper. It seemed he always just hired someone when he arrived at his destination, and he was perfectly willing to sit until someone came along. The heavy after-work traffic was flowing in front of the house now, drivers craning to look at the van, their interest piqued by this minor distraction in an otherwise ordinary drive home. Then a car turned out of the traffic into our lot. Minutes later, another. And another. Thirty minutes after the van's arrival, a crew of four men from our new church had hired on, the treasurer had arrived with the check, and the boxes had begun to pile up in our five-and-a-half rooms. Beds at Lee's folks' house that night had never looked so good!

All next day we unpacked. A steady stream of people flowed in and out (with shoes on) across the new rug. Food was brought in. We ate gingerly at the new dining-room table, wondering aloud how we would manage meals with the children and keep the rug clean. Obviously, a sheet of plastic would be required under the high chair.

Lee found the wooden letters for the bulletin board in front of the church and posted his sermon topic: Have Robe, Will

Travel. This brought more people to the door. And each time we stopped to talk. The next day was Saturday; we wanted our family together by Saturday night so we could all meet the church people on Sunday morning. We worked faster between visitors. We were ready to quit about ten o'clock Friday night when the final knock of the day came at the door.

There stood the district superintendent and his wife. "Just driving by and saw your sermon title. That's pretty good! I know you're going to do fine here." We offered them the couch while we sank down gratefully on packing boxes. "Can't stay. Just wanted to say welcome to the district. How's your office coming?" Lee took the cue and the three of them disappeared into the church. Not knowing how long they would be gone, I started to empty another box.

Half an hour later, Lee came back alone.

"That was really nice of them to come by, wasn't it?" The words came before I straightened up to look at him. His face reminded me of the day we had first seen our potato-cellar church. "What's wrong?"

"Nothing. Absolutely nothing. The D.S. just told me that five churches in this town are one too many, and this might just as well be the one to close down; that I should think about that. After all, the neighborhood is changing, we've got industry, the railroad yards, and the wash for the Los Angeles riverbed at our back. Well, he's wrong! This church is going to stay and *grow!*"

Sunday morning, with the shades carefully pulled on the bedroom side of the house (next to the front door of the church), I dressed the children in their best for their introduction to the congregation. The parking lot was filling up. I could hear people's voices punctuated by laughter and an occasional word or phrase. At five minutes before service time, I stepped out the front door with Tim in my arms, followed by Mark and Becky. I couldn't get off the porch. It was covered with children, jumping off, climbing over the railing, packed tightly on the steps.

Mark sized up the situation as only a seven-year-old could. "What are you doing on our front porch?" he asked the line of giggling girls on the steps.

"It's not *your* front porch," answered a pert curly-haired beauty as she jumped over the bushes into the yard. "It belongs to the church, and we can sit on it if we want! My mother said so."

A group of women stood nearby watching the scene as they chatted. One of them stepped toward me, introduced herself, and then said, "I'm from the choir, and we were wondering if it would be all right to practice in the living room on Sunday morning? It's the only place to practice while Sunday school classes are meeting." Shades of New Jersey bathrooms! And with a white rug yet. . . . At least by this time I'd learned to say, "Well, we'll see."

The church was full. The congregation responded well to Lee, and afterward, punch, cake, and coffee gave people time to talk and introduce themselves. Nothing about the morning indicated that the church should be closed. In fact, the image we carried back to the house was just the opposite: young families, children, hard-working people for whom the church could be central in their lives. But Lee thought about the words of the D.S. as he went about the task of settling in. One afternoon he came in with a broad smile.

"I've got it, Ruth!"

"Got what?"

"The right name for this church."

That's how *St. Fifth By-the-Wash* entered our private vocabulary.

## 2

By September it was obvious. The wall between the service porch and kitchen would have to go. We had developed a Saturday night ritual which clearly pointed to its removal: first bathe the kids, then the carpet. With rug cleaner and brush, scrub under the dining table, then the paths to the bedrooms, and finally the paths to the front door. Almost any Saturday night at eleven, I could be found on my hands and knees cleaning the rug.

Removing the wall would provide only a partial answer, but

even the chairman of the trustees agreed it should come out. Since he was also chairman of six other major committees in the church, his consent was rather crucial, to say the least.

By now Lee was beginning to understand the D.S.'s statement about closing this church. When four or five people are responsible for all the decisions—and usually exercise their power by voting *against* anything the minister might suggest—movement and growth are a little difficult. And the first thing Lee asked for—a part-time secretary—was unheard of!

Immediately Lee and our seven-office member tangled. The wall, the man could understand. It was tangible. And its removal to make the kitchen larger would protect their investment in carpet. But a secretary? Never!

On a hot September morning, three men appeared at the back door with sledgehammers. Others kept dropping by all day. I hung sheets between the kitchen and dining area, but soon a haze of plaster dust filled the whole house.

"Should have been done a long time ago," a voice commented through the dust and noise.

"Hmph! If you ask me, we should tear the whole thing down," came the reply. "Somebody said we should use it for Sunday school classes and get another house for the preacher."

"You kidding? I wouldn't let my kids go to Sunday school in this firetrap!" Pounding drowned out the voices. . . .

Stunned, I looked at my children playing on the living-room floor and thanked God they couldn't understand the meaning of such words. It was all right for us to *live* in this house, but it was too dangerous for *their* children, even for one hour on Sunday morning. Certainly it made sense to use the house for classes. They had done so for years, off and on, depending on the size of the minister's family. With all the space filled by our three children, they were feeling a little cramped—even with the choir practicing in the living room (with their shoes on) every Sunday morning.

By late afternoon the wall (and the men) were gone. A gaping hole in the linoleum and plaster marked its spot, but somehow it was a beautiful hole, for it represented a tiny corner of privacy where I would soon be able to feed my family without fear of criticism. But by nightfall, Tim, who had been marvelously healthy here in the city, was choked with bronchitis. Plaster dust was everywhere. With wheezing baby on one hip, I began vacuuming while Lee cleaned all the washable surfaces. This time it wasn't just because tomorrow was Sunday, but to eliminate the dust that had triggered this bronchial attack. But no matter—in a couple of weeks we'd have a finished kitchen, and life would settle back to normal—whatever that was. . . .

Wrong again! I had to admit it. We were *still* young and naive. We knew almost nothing about life, and even less about volunteer labor. Since the renovation included moving the washer and dryer, the plumber and electrician had to do their work first. This meant several days without water in the kitchen, since the plumber could come only at night—after he had already worked a full day. Certainly we weren't going to object to any delay. Then there were parts to be ordered. No problem—the church kitchen was only a few steps away, so we'd just move a few things over there and be completely out of the way while the work proceeded. . . . and proceeded. New pipes had to replace old ones. Plaster wire was required. Could anyone do plastering? Then there were the paint and the floor covering. And no point in not painting the ceiling and all the walls, right? And of course, the kitchen cupboards.

That's how it happened that I was in the church kitchen with one of the women when our seven-office member came striding across the social hall from Lee's study. "I don't know why we need a church secretary," he complained briskly. Then, covering the intensity of his words with a programmed smile, he finished, "I thought that was the minister's wife's job."

As though his smile were real, I laughed and countered, "That's funny. I didn't get a paycheck last week!" He never mentioned it to me again. . . . But the other woman heard.

October whizzed by, but the work crawled. Most of our food supplies were now in the church cupboards, and the kids must have thought we were living there. Toys that had been strewn through the living room and bedrooms now littered the social hall and backyard as well. Initial enthusiasm had waned as the project dragged on. Actually, it had been present only on wall-knocking-out day—the fun part. Putting things back into living shape wasn't nearly as interesting.

Meanwhile, the board met, responded to the words of the woman from the kitchen, and hired a secretary—and laughed about our living in the church. That was getting to be an ever more impossible feat, since with urging from Becky and Mark, Tim had begun to walk. Until then he had just climbed—to the top of the piano, the toilet tank—anything he could get to. With both feet steady, his climbing was less insistent, but since we were living in two places, he demanded increased watchfulness.

October faded into November. The plumber and electrician had finished their work—bless them!—and one man had stayed faithful (the man who didn't want his children "in this firetrap"). With him, we painted the walls and cupboards and finally moved back into the kitchen, a long ten weeks after the first sledgehammer blow. But most important had been the blow struck at the tight control of church decisions. Our faithful worker had been a borderline attender at the beginning of the project. By the end, he was a good friend and disgusted member. "So this is how things get done around here," he was heard to mutter. "Well, that's got to change!" We were sure he would see that it did.

Having discovered such a fine electrician, who also happened to love the church, Lee seized the opportunity to light the steeple. (Remember New Jersey?) The church sat at a curve in the street, so its lighted steeple could be seen from both directions. And our faithful kitchen worker came by one day with a beautiful handcrafted cross he had made from a sketch Lee had drawn one morning over coffee. It was exactly the focal point needed over the altar.

By December the church was full almost every Sunday. And true to form, Lee's world was expanding. First he followed a reference to a prison camp high on Mt. Wilson. On his day off, he would start up the mountain to minister to forgotten men, following a winding two-lane highway that rose above the timber line. He was paid barely enough to cover the travel costs, but it kept his ministry fresh. These people who had been set aside by society were a constant reminder to Lee that the world is not made just of churchgoers. And he was able to remind the church people that the message of Christ wasn't just for them.

In New Jersey, Lee had enjoyed the comradeship of the Lion's Club, recognizing that such contacts often open doors of service to people outside the church. In this town, the High-Noon Optimists extended an invitation to be their chaplain, and Lee accepted eagerly. Besides, our end of town needed help, and sometimes city decisions can be influenced more easily if one knows the people who make them. And through both ventures the congregation grew: Optimists and released prisoners found their way to our church.

Thanksgiving and Christmas brought food for others piled high on the altar, and a candlelight service of carols filled people's hearts. The congregation presented us with a stocking full of dollar bills! We had taken a cut in salary —down from $4,000—when we came to this church (the D.S. had explained that our mountain salary had been supplemented with an "increment" for living in the back country), so the Christmas gift was not only heartwarming but welcome.

In contrast to mountain cold and snow, this holiday season was warm and balmy, and our chilren were excited to be spending Christmas at their grandparents' house. At the end of the day Becky was hugging a Tiny Tears doll, Mark was roaring around with a Whamo truck, and Timmy needed only the ripping of paper to make him squeal with delight. Our cup was running over with blessings.

The phone rang the day after Christmas. The head of the conference committee on work projects wanted to know if Lee would like to take a team of boys to Africa next summer?

Would he? Just try to stop him! All he needed was the permission of the church board. . . .


3


Lee and I talked and talked. How could we present it to the board so they would say yes? This was not an ordinary request for a week or two—it was for a whole summer. And with Lee in Africa, I certainly wasn't going to stay alone in the house with total responsibility for three kids! I'd get someone to help drive and go to visit my grandmother in Kentucky and my parents in Michigan. That meant the house would stand empty while we were gone. We were so concerned with the Africa trip that we barely noticed when Becky began to sneeze and sniff. Then Mark got our attention with a full case of flu: chills, fever, cold, diarrhea—the works. Lee soon joined him.

By the time Tim began to cough, we had already planned a dinner at our house for the whole board. It would give those who hadn't seen the finished kitchen an opportunity to inspect it. And it would be our way to thank the board for their generosity at Christmas. And perhaps it would also be a good setting for breaking the news about Africa. Meanwhile, Tim had developed an abscessed ear and my head was beginning to hurt.

The Sunday before the dinner, church attendance told the story: an epidemic of flu was in full swing. But everyone just laughed and said they would be exposed wherever they were, so there was no need to cancel the dinner and meeting. Only Tim was still under medical care at that point, and except for lost sleep when he cried at night, we were managing. Thirty people had been invited. I tried to gauge the menu accordingly and imported dishes, silverware, and coffeepots from the church.

The day of the dinner arrived. I set a buffet table. The house was clean and the kids were scrubbed. Then the phone began to ring. "Sorry, I really want to come, but I'm afraid I've got the flu," a clogged voice would say. By the time the dinner hour chimed, eighteen souls in various degrees of unhealth had arrived. We ate, coughed, and blew our noses—mine was just beginning to run—and since we were all miserable, we could all laugh about it together.

In fact, we were so miserable that when Lee explained about his opportunity to take the conference team to Africa, it was a marvelous distraction (God's mysterious ways, again!). None of the board members had been there, few had traveled out of the state, and each began to spin daydreams about distant places. Nothing fazed them. They put together a salary agreement so the kids and I wouldn't starve, agreed to hire someone to fill in for the summer months, and cheered Lee's good fortune! We were amazed (oh we of little faith)!

As winter turned into spring, I began to wonder about having the sole responsibility for three small children. Becky was at the stage where she was quite expert at buttons, and several times she demonstrated her prowess by removing all her clothes while sitting on the front steps. Mark had begun to play at friends' houses occasionally, and I stayed constantly alert until he returned. And Tim was never still.

Meanwhile, Lee was so busy with church, prison, and Africa-team arrangements that he seldom noticed what was going on at home. He couldn't understand my distress when I was the only woman with small children at women's society meetings, or my humiliation when Becky filled her plate with spaghetti at one of their dinners, then promptly spilled it down her front and all over the floor—just missing the immaculate shoes of one member. Their debates about whether to hire a sitter for meetings made me uncomfortable, for it was almost always my children who needed to be cared for; yet I was expected to be there. Most of the other mothers attended the evening group and left their children with fathers or sitters. When I complained, Lee assured me that no one really cared, that I was overreacting—until the day he stayed home with the kids while I went to the meeting.

You remember the order: parking lot/house/church. Lee had a project underway, and the uncarpeted floor of the boys' bedroom was the only place he could work without concern for sawdust. It was simply too cold to work outside. The women had invited a special speaker, so after lunch we gathered in the sanctuary. As we began to sing, Lee began to saw. By the time the program chairperson rose to introduce the speaker, Lee was pounding away. Her first sentence was, "Would somebody in the back please go over to the parsonage and ask the preacher to be quiet?" I slid down in my seat. No wonder one minister had left six weeks before conference! Our seven-office man had asked him when he was "going to get out of the parsonage so we can get in there and fix it up?" The poor man had left that very day; two days later, all his belongings, wife, and children had also disappeared. It was more than obvious that the location of the parsonage proved difficult for both congregation and minister.

Lee was furious. Shades of the New Jersey lock! "This is our house. I have a right to do what I need to do in it! I wasn't making that much noise. . . ." He cooled down eventually. I was the one who hid it in my heart. From that time on, whenever people were in the church (which was most of the time), I found myself telling the children to be quiet; or I stopped playing the piano; or turned down the TV.

When the weather warmed and the dining-room windows on the parking-lot side were open, people called out to us—carried on conversations through the screens—no matter that we were having dinner or entertaining guests. At night I would sometimes have the uncomfortable feeling that people were listening at the windows.

And they came to the door. They were not accustomed to having a secretary and a pastor who worked in the church office. First they knocked at the parsonage door. The path on the not-quite-so-white rug from kitchen to door grew darker. Scrubbing was having less effect all the time . . . especially since an adult Sunday school class had also begun to meet at the house. Frequently when the choir was rehearsing, I would see the director look at the carpet with a critical eye. He was the one who had picked it out, and I knew he thought I wasn't giving it proper care. I cringed inside. Outside, I just kept singing or smiling, trying not to offend, trying to be a good minister's wife. After all, like most women of my generation, my future was tied to my husband's success. . . .

Nevertheless, it was with great anticipation that we marked the days until Lee would leave for Africa and I for the Midwest. A nurse had answered my ad for a traveling companion. Both of us were happy with her, and about this chance for my parents to get to know their grandchildren.

But a call from Mark's teacher dampened our enthusiasm. What was she to do? Mark wasn't finishing his lessons, he seemed distracted, indifferent. Was anything unusual happening at home? Armed with the knowledge of Lee's impending trip, she discovered that our poor little second-grader had seen a TV news program about a massive tidal wave in Africa that had killed hundreds of people. Now Mark was sure his daddy would be killed by a tidal wave. Our nightly dinner conversations were quickly scaled down to specifics about travel, places, and activities, so that the children would understand.

Lee could scarcely contain himself as departure time approached. He and the four young college men were setting out for a place called Kinandu in the Belgian Congo. What more adventure could a young minister ask for? If only his passport would come back from the Jordanian consulate . . . they had kept it almost a month.

The final week arrived. Lee was packed and ready—except or two things. His passport still hadn't been returned. Frantic calls had finally turned up a reason: everyone at the whole consulate had gone on vacation! The second missing item was equally important. He had not received the conference check that would pay all the expenses for his team and a team of older adults who were also going to Africa.

By asking a Congressman to vouch for him, the passport office issued Lee a temporary document. But the check didn't arrive until Friday afternoon. They were to leave on Sunday. Where do you go to cash a $5,000 check after five o'clock on Friday afternoon?

A memory flashed through my mind: "If it's the Lord's will, you'll have clear sailing. But if it isn't, you'll have trouble all the way!" We were still young. We hadn't learned to listen. . . .

4

No one had that kind of money—at least, no one *we* knew! Lee started calling banks, but in those days, they were all closed on Saturday. Next he tried the merchants he knew in the church and in the Optimists. No luck. Worse yet, there would be no way to change the money into traveler's checks if he *did* have it—and he *had* to have it. The other team leader was counting on *his* half, too.

"Lee, why don't you call your dad? Maybe he could put the

money together, or maybe he knows someone who could."

"My dad?" he replied incredulously. "He wouldn't keep that kind of money in the house—even if he had that much."

But there really weren't any options. Lee's dad was a grading contractor and never knew how or when people might pay him. On the phone, Lee explained his plight. To his amazement, Pop told him to hold on while he looked. Sure enough! After calling all over Los Angeles, it was his own father who had no trouble cashing the check. A fluke had saved us: several old bills had been paid late Friday in cash. Pop was as relieved that the money was out of the house as Lee was to take it.

With much excitement—and the money stuffed inside Lee's clothes, shoes, and camera case—the two teams left for their first destination—New York City. From there they would go their separate ways. On the plane, the two team leaders discovered that neither of them had been given a budget by the conference; neither knew what kinds of expenses they might incur. Hastily, they drew up an expense sheet: where they were going, how many flights per person, hotels, food. Everything was pure guesstimate. And the money was not in a few clean $100 bills, but rumpled $1s, $5s, $10s—the kind construction men carry around in their pockets. Obviously, there was no place on the plane to lay out such money for counting and dividing.

Off the plane in New York, they headed for the men's restroom. With team members standing guard in a circle, the two Methodist ministers got down on their knees (a most appropriate posture) and sorted the money into piles. Phrases such as "You take that one, I'll keep this one" floated upward. To the innocent restroom visitor, the scene must have looked like the biggest crap game in New York. Finally, for safety's sake, the money was subdivided and stashed on each person. If one were robbed, the others would still have money. With this accomplished, Lee's team boarded a plane for Europe. Now the Africa saga could begin in earnest.

Meanwhile, back at the ranch—oops, parsonage—Lee's regular passport had arrived in the mail. I immediately forwarded it via an airplane pilot to an address in Athens, Greece, where the team would be stopping.

The white station wagon sat on the parking lot, packed and ready. Lee's dad had helped me secure the luggage on top with electrical wire when we ran out of rope. It looked bizarre but was sturdy. The refrigerator was emptied except for breakfast makings, and our ice chest was filled for the trip. As soon as my nurse/driving companion arrived the next morning, we would leave. With tearful goodbyes and many admonitions to be careful, Mom and Pop left. "Be sure to call us in the morning before you go, so we'll know everything's all right," were their last words. Of course I would.

We were all up early the next morning, excited and eager to leave. At 7:30 the phone rang. It was the nurse. She was sorry not to have called me sooner, but her father was very ill, and she had hoped he would be better this morning so she could still go, but it really was impossible, and she hoped this wasn't going to inconvenience me.

I stared at the phone in disbelief. Thirty minutes before we had agreed to leave on a cross-country trip with three small children, she had called to say she wasn't going! I looked at the car on the parking lot, packed and ready. The kids were dancing around, anticipating the trip to their "other grandma's." The refrigerator was empty. Mom and Pop's words rang in my head: "Call us . . . "—I wouldn't dare!

Hanging up the receiver, I picked up my purse, made a last tour of the house to be sure we had everything, and before I could change my mind, the house was locked and we were in the car, headed for the freeway and parts East. Maybe I would call Lee's folks from some distant desert town.

As we left the city behind and entered the outskirts of wide expanses of desert, I thought of Lee's warnings. "If you have car trouble, hail a truck driver. They usually know what to do or can radio for help. . . . The car's in good shape, Ruth, but don't take any chances. If it overheats in the desert, stop and let it cool off." He had given the car a complete check before he left. That was reassuring. In the rearview mirror I could see Mark and Becky playing happily. Tim was asleep in his car-bed, for what I hoped would be a long morning nap.

"This is really crazy, Ruth," my head told me. "Starting out alone across the United States with three kids—ages 7, 3½, and barely 2. You've never driven more than four hours at a stretch in your life. And you know you can't call Mom and Pop until you're a long way from here, or they'll be worried silly. You ought to turn around and *go back*." I couldn't. There was nothing to go back to! My husband was on his way to Africa, and my house was under the charge of the young seminarian who was taking care of the church. Nobody knew I was alone, and it was best this way.

The sun rose higher. We stopped for lunch at a roadside park. Desert winds helped cool us a little, and the freedom to run eased the many questions—beginning with "How much farther, Mother?" Of course we had pulled off the road several times for drinks of water and diaper changes. At this rate, it would take us a long time to get across the country.

The sun stared mockingly into the car windows. Becky and Tim were both asleep when I saw the heat indicator begin to rise. I slowed down. Maybe with all the luggage on top, the motor was working overtime. Five-and-a-half hours from home, I wheeled gratefully into another rest stop as the peg hit the top and steam started to rise from the radiator.

In Athens, Lee was making daily inquiries. Had his passport come? The team stalled as long as they could, and that was just long enough. Lee had *two* valid passports when they landed at Elizabethville. When the five young Americans entered the airport gates, they were bewildered to see lines of people waiting, shoving and pushing to board the plane they had just left. Curiously, they were the only people who had gotten off. Preoccupied with traveling and sightseeing, they had not heard the news: the Congo was boiling with turmoil as the date for its independence from Belgium approached, just five days hence. All the people clamoring to leave were white; so were Lee and his four team members. . . .

By the time someone had come to my rescue in the desert, and a service station attendant had removed the thermostat from the car because it was "the best thing to do in the desert," I was ready to call it a day. We were only six hours from home. We could still go back; Lee's folks would take us in. As I put the children to bed in the motel and pored over the maps and the miles ahead of us, I decided not to call Mom and Pop until the next night. The car was in good shape. If I could drive eight hours a day, we'd reach my Kentucky grandmother by Friday, stay there a week, then go on to Michigan. Mark was assuming responsibility for the younger two and seemed to be enjoying it. With his help, I'd go on.

As Lee's team was settling into the mission station at Kinandu, the kids and I were heading across the Texas panhandle. I had finally called Mom and Pop and told them we were traveling by ourselves. Other than the overheated thermostat the first day and the replacment of two tires the second, we were doing just fine. The car hummed along beautifully; the children had settled into a traveling routine.

We checked into a motel for the third night and went next door to supper. After paying the check I turned around,my eyes suddenly riveted on Mark. He was ghost-white and trembling.

"What's wrong, Mark?" He didn't answer. He just pointed out the window. To my great relief, I saw a magnificent display of Texas lightning flash across the sky. The poor California kid had never seen the sky *do* that!

In Africa, the team had been apprised of what was happening. In the streets, people were selling empty boxes, supposedly filled with "independence"; a huge parade was being organized in Elizabethville to celebrate the nation's liberty. And blacks were threatening whites openly. The team members were assured they would be safe if they were known as part of the mission. The day of independence arrived, and when the parade was over the Boy Scouts continued marching almost all day. How threatened can you feel with Boy Scouts marching around, shouting about their new nation? Lee's greatest worry was his family.

He had received my first letter, telling him that I had left by myself and outlining the thermostat and tire troubles that had been successfully handled. No other mail came, and there was no way for us to contact each other. At night he would lie on his cot and mentally go over the car, piece by piece, to reassure himself. But his worries vanished during the day, for there were forty thousand bricks to be shaped and fired for a new schoolroom. And while the bricks were baking, the Africans taught the team members the Swahili language and African dances. And they taught the Africans the Virginia Reel. Tales of killings drifted into the mission station, but their area was peaceful.

Fortunately, I didn't know what was happening in the Congo. Besides, when the car caught fire in the middle of the Great Plains, I really wasn't thinking about Lee. The kids had been restless and quarrelsome all day, tired of being cooped up in the car, and I was delighted when they finally settled down for a nap—even Mark. But now smoke was pouring from under the hood. Pulling onto the narrow shoulder, I turned off the ignition, grabbed Tim and his thumb-sucking blanket, and plopped him on the bank, well away from the car. Mark, wakened by our sudden stop, jumped out with Becky and kept watch on the two younger ones.

Cautiously, I lifted the hood. Tiny flames were threading their way along the electrical wires. Tim's blanket quickly smothered them. It never occurred to me that the gasoline might explode. (Shades of the New Jersey furnace!) I just knew that my kids and I were on a roadbank in the middle of nowhere—not a house in sight—and the car obviously was not going any farther. But we were safe, at least for the moment.

Now what? "Hail a truck" had been Lee's words. Coming along the highway was a farm truck. I waved the blanket with all my might. The driver pulled to a stop.

"Just helped another lady about five miles back," he began. "What seems to be the trouble?" Bless him! He didn't condemn me for dragging my kids across the country or for being so foolish as to undertake such a trip. He just looked at the problem, traced the still smoking wire and said, "Well, I could probably fix this good enough to get you to the next town. They've got a garage there. Only problem is, I haven't got any wire."

Wire! My eyes went to the luggage rack. "Would this work?" I pointed.

"Sure would. Lucky you got that on there. Not many folks

use wire to tie down luggage. . . ." Luck? Or God? An hour later I pulled into the garage at the next town.

"How far you going, lady?" asked the mechanic after inspecting our new wiring job. "Kentucky? Might just as well leave it the way it is till you get there. Looks like a good job to me." Time for a break; the kids and I romped in the park. Surely nothing else could happen—and even if it did, God was certainly looking after us.

In Africa, news of violence was coming in regularly now, but the team had come to do a job, and they decided to stay until the missionaries told them to leave. The mission station did seem to be protected. Besides firing brick and teaching the Africans how to maintain the agricultural tractors the church had supplied, the team wanted to complete a *real* job, something permanent. Every year the flood waters rose to wash away the only bridge into the compound, and during conflict, the road was essential for escape. The bridge could be their big project.

There was a major problem with building a bridge that would hold against floods, however. It required a pier in the middle of the river—and the river was full of bilharzi, tiny parasites that bore their way into the skin, live and multiply in the body, then exit via the eyes. No one wanted to work in *that* water! So the five Americans, watched by incredulous Africans who wouldn't go near the water, began dumping dirt into the river to build a coffer dam of sorts. Soon there was a walkway to the middle of the river. Realizing they weren't going to get wet, the Africans began to help, and in no time at all, they had an area wide enough to sink a shaft through to bedrock. Here, protected, they would build the pier. So Lee headed across the old bridge to Elizabethville for lumber and tools.

The city had become a war zone. Burned cars littered the streets. The lumberyard was vacant. Lee took what he needed and left an IOU at the idle cash register. With the new tools, he cut steel from some of the abandoned vehicles to use in strengthening the bridge pier. Gunshots sounded in the distance. He must hurry back to the station, but first he'd check the post office. Maybe there would be word from his family. Nothing. On the way back to the mission station, he saw piles of mail lying in the ditches. . . .

Sunday morning, I was determined that *today* we would make it to my grandmother's home. The day was intermittently rainy, the roads narrow and winding, making the Kentucky landscape seem almost mystical. The kids' happy laughter filled the car, for they knew we would soon arrive. (They'd also think twice about agreeing to go see Grandma again!) We were now about three hours from the end of our journey.

Suddenly my eye was caught by the heat gauge. The indicator was completely past the hot zone. I pulled quickly to the side, got out, and lifted the hood. There was no steam, nothing seemed unduly warm. Back inside, I looked again. The indicator was still on its side—and so were those of all the other instruments—oil, gas, electrical. I had lost them all. Poor car! It was just going to give up and die! I laughed right out loud.

A tiny cafe with two gas pumps was just ahead, and since now I wouldn't know how much gas was in the tank, and Kentucky's blue laws kept most businesses closed on Sunday, I knew I had better fill up. And maybe somebody there could tell me what had happened to my instrument panel.

A gangly young man approached the car in a lurching saunter, put his elbow on the open window frame and drawled, "Fill it up, ma'am?" His eyes searched the car.

"If you would, please." I watched him in my rearview mirror as he started the pump, looked at the license plate, then walked all the way around the car and back to the window.

"Where you comin' from, ma'am?" Space hung between each word.

"California."

"All alone!?" His question was more an expression of disbelief.

"Well, my three children are with me."

He walked back to disengage the pump, then returned for the money. As he counted out my change, he shook his head slowly. "Ma'am," he stopped to study the horizon, "I wouldn't even go out of *Ken-tucky* by myself."

No need to ask him about the gauges. It would only convince him never to leave even the station in his lifetime.

5

The paper fell to the floor, its red banner headline consuming the room: *MINISTER LOST IN CONGO.* No one in California had heard from Lee. They knew only that the American ambassador had ordered all Americans out of the Congo. He and his team had not come across the border. My eyes scanned the note from Lee I held in my hand. I went to the telephone.

The church secretary answered. "There's really nothing wrong," I assured her. "I've been getting mail right along." Actually, I hadn't heard from Lee in three days, but that wasn't unusual. "Yes, I'm sure he's fine. He's at the mission station in Kinandu." She thanked me for calling, said she would notify the paper, but somehow she seemed not to believe me. I chuckled to myself about the greeting card I had impulsively mailed Lee two days before. It would be fun to see his face when he opened it. And putting the green stamps that I got with its purchase inside would surely make it a better joke. . . .

If only I could have seen behind those headlines, I would not have been so calm.

At Kinandu, Lee and his team were busy with the bridge. The distant gunfire was becoming more frequent, and daily nearer. In the middle of the river, rocks, steel from the burned cars, and concrete were disappearing into the dirt form. Protected from the water, the workers moved rapidly. Only once did fear strike, and then not because of guns, but the dreaded bilharzi. A tool fell into the water. Without it, they could not continue, and the road to Elizabethville was now closed. Lee made the fastest dive of his life (he says he came up dry), and the tool was back in use.

Almost two weeks had passed since the ambassador's order to leave had been received. Two young women, on a special two-year missionary assignment in Elizabethville, had fled to the relative safety of Kinandu just before the road had closed, so there were seven Americans now in hiding. The Africans assured them they would tell them when it was time to leave. . . .

The team had finished a long work day and were feeling good. The pier was strong, the beams for the roadbed sturdy, and the surface planks almost all in place. Lee was the last to luxuriate in the shower-from-a-barrel they had rigged up. Just then one of the Africans came to him. "It is time to go." Thinking he meant "go to dinner," Lee continued to enjoy the cool water. The African persisted, and suddenly it dawned . . . it was time to *go!* Time to leave the Congo! The five young men and the two women, with all their luggage, piled into the mission wagon and started for Elizabethville. On the outskirts of the city an African guard called them to a halt, asking for passports. It was obvious he could not read—he held the passports upside down. It was just as obvious that the ancient American-made submachine gun he held was operative. Only the words on the side of the wagon saved them: Mission Methodiste. The guard waved them on.

At Methodist headquarters in Elizabethville, Lee faced the problem of finding a way out of the country. Flights had been discontinued. If they could reach Old Umtali Mission, near Salisbury in Southern Rhodesia (now Zimbabwe), perhaps they could still complete a summer of work for the church. The only way out of the Congo, however, was by car, and that was hazardous because of the fighting. Besides, the only operative vehicle was the mission station wagon, and that was needed at Elizabethville. Late that night Lee was reading at the table, the only one still awake and with a light burning. A jeep roared past; the building was cut through by machine-gun fire just above his head. It really *was* time to get out. There was one chance . . . an old abandoned station wagon. If he could just repair it in time. . . .

Lee worked almost nonstop for twenty-four hours. Parts were easily available at the local auto-parts store, whose doors had been left unlocked in the owner's hasty exit. Another IOU was left by an idle cash register. Team members helped with the car, scrounged parts, or simply disappeared to sleep. No one felt safe. No one *was* safe. And at last, the car ran!

While the others were packing, Lee made one last trip to the post office. The building sat in the middle of town, the open ends of the mailboxes facing outside. Lee could see the mission box from the building across the street where he had taken cover. An envelope was in it! If he ran across the open space quickly, perhaps he could get it out before somebody took a shot at him. Reaching the box, he snatched the letter and was halfway back before a rifle shot tore the air. He covered the last few yards on his belly. Crouching in a doorway, he saw the familiar handwriting. At last he would know what was happening to his family. With trembling fingers, he ripped open the envelope.

In his hands was a long slim greeting card. A floozy-looking overweight woman—obviously a streetwalker—stared back at him, an impertinent flower stuck in her red hair. HEY, BIG BOY! shouted the message. Unbelieving, he opened the card: YOU FORGOT YOUR GREEN STAMPS! A sheet of green stamps was pasted below the words. At the bottom was written: "I love you. Ruth." No message, no letter, nothing. It was the only thing I sent to Africa that whole summer that got through.

The road toward the border was like most African roads in 1960: two paved strips with a high dirt crown in the middle. As long as only one vehicle was on the road, driving was relatively safe; but when two cars met, each had to move to the side with only two wheels remaining on the pavement. Such construction was great for tropical rains . . . driving on those roads was another matter.

The seven Americans, in their old station wagon piled high with luggage and souvenirs, breathed a collective sigh of relief as they crossed into Northern Rhodesia. Lee fell into an exhausted sleep, slumped in the middle of the back seat. Now it was just a matter of time until they could make their way to the refugee camp at Salisbury. The driver, as tired as the others, saw the cement truck approaching. In his weariness, he reacted as an American and moved to the right side of the road—directly in line with the British left-side driver. Each swerved to miss the other. The wheels of the huge truck climbed over the car's hood. Doors burst open; people flew in all directions—except Lee. He was tossed forward just in time to catch the full impact of an exploding windshield in his face. The curled end (what had it hit?) of an African spear—a souvenir—stopped two inches from the back of his head.

The sound of the grinding crash brought a woman running from a nearby ranch with ammonia and clean cloths. Her name was Rut (*Ruth* in our language!), and she informed them that "she had seen lots worse as a nurse in the London blitz." Insisting that Lee drink sips of water mixed with ammonia to keep from passing out, she straddled his chest and began to pull pieces of glass from his face (shades of Bali dancers!), dousing the cuts with more ammonia and carefully taping each one closed. The other passengers were jostled and bruised, but otherwise unharmed. Gathering up what remained of their luggage and bidding goodbye to their worthless car, they gratefully accepted an offered ride into Salisbury.

At the refugee camp, the team presented a problem to the British Rhodesian government. While they were refugees from the Congo and entitled to care, they were neither English nor African, but American, and moreover, one of the young women was black. In an apartheid country, she could not be housed in their hotel, even though she was an American. They would all be fed, thanks to the Red Cross, but *she,* at least, would have to sleep elsewhere.

The hotel dining room, with typical English dignity, maintained a strict dress code—jackets and ties absolutely required for men. Since most of their belongings had been left by the roadside, the five men could not enter. A guest, seeing their plight, disappeared and soon returned with five ties and coats of various sizes. They put these on over their soiled and sweaty T-shirts, and the motley crew was then allowed to sit at the linen- and crystal-covered tables, with a waiter standing at each elbow to meet their every need. Elegant menus were presented.

It had been more than a month since they had eaten anything but African food. Saliva flowed as each carefully made a selection, knowing that permission had been given for them to order anything they wanted, compliments of the government. When the waiter turned to take the order of the last team member, the young man smiled, handed the menu to the waiter and said, "That will do just fine." They brought him everything on the menu. And, as the saying goes, he "ate the *whole* thing"!

Lodging was a different matter. Since their black companion could not stay in the hotel, and the group obviously was becoming a problem to the camp's commandant, they offered to go on to Old Umtali. The offer was gratefully accepted.

Reaching the mission where the women would remain, a decision was made. After all they had been through, it might be more advantageous for the team to see the beauty of Africa than to work, so with a loaned van, the five set off to retrace the steps of Livingston, camping in the bush at night beside a fire to ward off curious animals. Had Lee forgotten about the gasoline that had soaked into his jeans while he was repairing the car? One night deep in the back country, a spark flew. With a whoosh, the pantleg caught. Instinctively Lee started to run, but was saved by the quick action of two team members who tackled him and, with their own bodies, smothered the flames—but not before the leg was covered with second- and third-degree burns. It was the next night before they found the wavering lights of a bush mission station—medical help at last!

With Lee's leg bandaged from foot to hip and a cane to help him walk, they now made their way through the back country, getting treatment where they could, always facing the threat of infection and blood poisoning.

A white woman came up beside Lee as he hobbled along a road some days afterward. "Is that what they did to you in the Congo?" she asked.

As if in answer, an African fell into step with him a while later: "In the Congo, they hurt your leg. Here we will kill you!"

Upon their return to Umtali, two of the team members announced their decision: they were going back to Kinandu to finish the bridge. Lee advised against it, but they were of age and adamant. So the remaining money was divided into five parts, enough to make sure each would reach home, and the other two, with Lee, left by plane for Cairo.

In Cairo, Lee proposed another idea. Instead of flying directly to Vienna, why not go up to Turkey—to Istanbul—to see the famed Santa Sophia cathedral, and then to Vienna? After all, they might never be in this part of the world again. The remaining two team members had but one thought in mind by this time—*home*. Lee bade them goodbye, saw their plane ascend, and set out with his cane to experience the Middle East. But first he must find a doctor for the leg that was now swollen and weeping.

The treatment was always the same: unwrap the bandages with the still-clinging flesh, then peel away the crusted skin in long strips. Antibiotic creams and new bandages finished the torture. But Lee was determined to see this part of the world, explore its streets and its pyramids. While exploring one of these, a guide took him deep inside, then threatened to leave unless he was given more money. A ring, bought from a street vendor late at night, turned out to be glass in the daylight. Other trinkets for the family filled his pockets.

But the leg was beginning to win. Also, after he had flown on to Istanbul, only to find Santa Sophia closed, he discovered that he had contracted a miserable case of Egyptian dysentery. And there was no commercial flight leaving Turkey in the next few days. A private pilot overheard Lee's anguished pleading at the ticket counter. He was flying to Vienna in his own plane. Would Lee like to come along? On such chance decisions, lives turn. . . .

The plane was over Hungary when it began to lose oil, and Budapest was a welcome airport. Lee, however, was *not* a welcome visitor. He was behind the Iron Curtain; American citizens were forbidden. But that did not occur to him as he painfully climbed out of the cockpit. His interest was caught by what seemed to be a line of C-47s. Lee did what any American tourist would do—he took a picture. Two guards appeared. Each grabbed one of his arms; they took his camera, passport, wallet, belt, and the small suitcase he was carrying. In minutes he was en route to solitary confinement in a Budapest prison, unsure of what his crime might be.

Reasoning that his best bet might be a connection with former President Harry Truman (he *is* a fourth cousin), each time the guard walked by, Lee would push himself as tall as possible on his one good leg and call out, "I am a TRUMAN." Later he added "WALLACE Truman." If they hadn't heard of one, perhaps they knew of the other. Between calls, he rested his always throbbing leg.

The next morning the key turned in the lock. Lee followed the guard to a car, was whisked to the airport, given his belongings, and told to board a waiting plane. Swinging his crippled leg up the steps, he turned at the last possible moment—and took another picture! He didn't even know whether there was film in the camera. But not until the plane was airborne did he realize—he was the *only* passenger. The sight of the Vienna airport was most welcome. . . .

The man who finally disembarked at Detroit walked right up to me before I knew him. His bushy red beard hid still-healing scars. His body was gaunt from dysentery. His cane supported the London-rebandaged leg. Only his arms and warm lips told me it was Lee.

Mark was wrong. A tidal wave didn't destroy Lee. But everything else almost did!

6

Back in California, everyone wanted to hear the story—or at least that's how it seemed to the kids and me. The newspaper article published after an interview stated that Lee and four young college students had built a bridge "comparable to the Golden Gate in San Francisco." Lee quickly learned not to joke with reporters. He had just naturally assumed that anyone would know that five people couldn't produce a span like that. . . .

And the church was waiting. It had basked in publicity throughout the summer as the whole city read the banner headlines. Now that the minister was home, only slightly the worse for wear, there was work to do. It was time to turn in the wool rags they had been collecting for a *reversible* sanctuary carpet. When one side wore out, it only needed to be flipped over! Lee was squeezing calling, preaching, prison work, administration—and now speaking engagements—into the same amount of hours. He thrived on it! It never occurred to him to drop anything, even though he was with his family less and less.

Construction was in Lee's blood now. The church needed a new porch to shade the worshipers from the hot summer sun. And a narthex with cool green plants on one side would increase the feeling of calm and quiet as people entered. Church members could do the work themselves to keep the cost down, and all Lee had to do was sell the idea . . . and help with the work. Soon the sounds of hammers and saws, concrete mixers, shouts and laughter, were added to the bedroom side of the house. It was hard to get our youngest two to take naps. But Lee was right. It really did add to the church.

All the time Lee had been in Africa, I had been thinking. Did I really want to do what I had vowed when I was sixteen—have four children before I turned thirty? I would look at our three and think our family was big enough, but then I'd recall all the times we had talked about having four children. Certainly from a practical standpoint, we couldn't afford another child. But from an idealistic view, four *were* what we (and I) had always planned. I decided that somehow I would feel incomplete—that a goal had been left unfinished—if we didn't have all four. *(Insanity comes in many forms!)*

So it was that one morning a few months later, I left Lee to supervise Becky and Tim while I went off to the doctor's office for my pregnancy checkup. When I returned two hours later, Lee was frantic. Tim was gone! While helping Becky dress, Lee had told two-and-a-half-year-old Tim to go ride his tricycle. Lee had meant "on the parking lot," but obviously Tim had other places in mind. Lee began to scour the neighborhood. Two women, members of the church, already were out looking. The police only laughed and said he was probably just in another yard. We couldn't convince them that he had never been in another yard—he was simply too young!

With Becky and Mark, I waited. Others had joined the search now, and the phone and doorbell rang with reports: not in this neighborhood; not here; we haven't seen him. The clock dragged on toward noon: Tim had been gone for three hours! The squad car came by again, and this time they agreed to keep an eye out for him. To say we were all praying is almost irrelevant. *Of course,* we were praying!

A tired but grinning Tim finally came home, brought by the two women who had searched all day. They had found him covered with chocolate ice cream, bought by a woman who spotted him about to cross the main thoroughfare of the city, still riding his tricycle, at almost three in the afternoon. Afterward, through sightings of neighbors, we were able to trace his path through almost four miles of the city, across many busy streets. Lee would never tell Tim to "go ride your tricycle" again. And quietly I wondered—*four* children? I could only imagine what the parishioners were thinking.

As winter brought the old familiar ice patches and fog, the weekly trips to the prison camp became more hazardous. One night visibility forced Lee to creep down the mountain. Seized suddenly by an unnatural compulsion to stop, he got out to see where he was. Only a few feet beyond the car was the edge of an unfenced passing turnout. He was completely off the road. It was long past midnight when he arrived home, having driven with the door open in order to see the pavement. But he loved the prisoners. Not until the following year when the district superintendent insisted he must either do prison work or care for the local church—but not both—did he give up his weekly trips. I was secretly glad. Maybe it was selfish, but I—we—needed him too.

Whenever the occasion of an African speech was to be an evening dinner and we could afford a sitter, I went along. It was fun to bask in my husband's glory (we were still very young!), to put on a special dress, to *feel* special. And I began to understand that people thought Lee and his team had done something very extraordinary. Since we had lived through it, the experience was just another event in our lives—the "norm." But both of us were genuinely surprised when he was named Optimist of the Year and then nominated for an Outstanding Young Men of America selection. He wasn't chosen for that elite group, but for us the nomination was exciting enough. And in the fashion of the day, I thought surely I had "hitched my wagon to a star."

That feeling lasted only until the next church board meeting. Because Lee thought a homey atmosphere made for better meetings, the board had begun to meet at the house (poor rug!). As quietly as possible, I would go about cleaning up the kitchen, then slip into the boys' bedroom and read to the kids so they would go noiselessly to bed.

We were midway in one of their favorite stories one night, when a voice in the living room began to rise louder and louder. I recognized it as that of our seven-office member. Through the last year, he had steadily been replaced by other people until now he held only one major job. As you might guess, this hadn't set too well. And now his anger was coming out—in the middle of a board meeting. I tried to keep my voice even as I continued to read, but my stomach was knotting up. It went into an absolute spasm moments later when I heard a second voice shouting back at the first. It was my husband—the pastor—Lee! The minister isn't supposed to shout! I read faster. Back and forth went the voices, then gradually they tapered off. Quiet talk and laughter followed. In the bedroom I wasn't laughing. My stomach was too tense.

With the children bedded down, I waited out the meeting, imagining all the terrible things that might happen because of Lee's outburst. People would talk, criticize, stop coming to church, maybe even ask for a new minister (talk about being paranoid!). When the door closed behind the last member, I rushed into the living room. "What on earth were you shouting about, Lee? I can't believe you did that!"

He walked calmly into the kitchen and took a long drink of water. "Nothing, really. I just decided that he was used to shouting to get his way and that the only language he would understand was someone shouting back. So I did. And it worked. He left friendly and happy." I knew then I would never understand people—or the ministry.

What I *did* understand was that Lee was still making speeches (he would finally give 254 of them) and that I was daily becoming more immobile as the birth of our fourth child approached. We were beginning our third year at this church when Lee came in one day very excited. He had been asked to speak at the morning worship service of a quite large church whose pastor he held in great respect. This was a very special invitation.

The young man who had filled our pulpit the summer before agreed to come again that Sunday morning. Lee, who normally gave his Africa speech by heart, set about preparing a mission *sermon* that included some of his experiences— quite a different approach. And it had to be good.

The week was hot and windy. Dust swirled up from the parking lot and settled in all available crevices. On Saturday, Lee rehearsed his message carefully and made sure his robe was in its carrier. Everything was in readiness. Sunday he was up early. Certainly this was no time to be late. Allowing himself thirty minutes more than enough time, he climbed into the white station wagon and turned the key. Nothing happened. Several more times he tried. He checked the battery with his meter. It was hopeless. The battery was dead. And the clock was ticking.

We ran through the list of people from whom he might borrow a car; his secretary topped the list. Another ten minutes passed before her familiar coupe pulled up out front. To save time at the other end of his journey, Lee had donned his pulpit robe, and dressed thus he ran to the car, thanked her, and started to climb in. She was almost a foot shorter than he and sat on a fiber-covered wire cushion. This he tossed into the back seat and drove away, dust swirling.

Lee arrived at the church just in time to step into the procession, still putting on his stole. The person behind him stepped closer and began to dust him off furiously. The window of the secretary's car had been open during that windy week, and now the perfect imprint of the wire cushion was transferred to the back of Lee's robe. As he walked through the door of the sanctuary, he could only hope that any remaining dust was not visible to the congregation.

During the opening liturgies and hymns, Lee refocused his mind on the sermon. Calmed, he stood to preach. He could see the people were interested in his message, and he leaned across the pulpit to make an important point. With a crash, the shelf inside the pulpit fell to the floor and with it, the controls for the sound system. One side panel collapsed, then another. (God certainly knows how to keep us humble!) When the pieces had stopped falling and rolling, Lee surveyed the debris. Grinning, he broke the stunned silence with, "I certainly don't guarantee the safety of anyone sitting under a chandelier. . . ."

Sometimes God speaks in a still small voice. *Or* in a rattling, crashing pulpit. Maybe—just maybe—it was time to put Africa to rest.


7


It was a hot July day when Nathan decided to complete our family. His father rushed home from a meeting to take me to the hospital, went back to the meeting, then returned to the hospital in time to greet our third son. Mark, Becky, and Tim were waiting eagerly for Nate and me when we arrived home two days later. The only problem was that I also brought home a minor infection. Two weeks later, it flared into a full-blown kidney attack . . . after doctors' office hours, naturally.

Lee finally got the doctor on the phone and described my symptoms. She knew of a pharmacy still open and would call in a prescription, but cautioned Lee that this medicine was powerful. Minutes later, as the pharmacist handed Lee the small package, he commented, "This is strong stuff." I took the medicine.

First I noticed that the top of my head felt dizzy, a most strange sensation. Then my vision began to fade in and out, and suddenly I couldn't get my breath. Gasping, I called to Lee. "I feel as if I'm dying." As I struggled to breathe, part of me seemed to be off to one side, very alert, very calm, making observations about the rest of me. That part knew that if I stopped fighting for breath, I would be dead—yet very peacefully alive. It was tempting. But from some other part of me came the awareness that I had three children and a new baby to care for. I must keep breathing.

Out of another remote distance came a siren, then hands

lifting me. I heard but could not respond. I knew I had arrived at a hospital; voices spun around my head. "Can't get a blood pressure reading." "Keep trying." Oxygen flowed into my lungs and I felt totally quiet inside. "This is why I'll never be a G.P.," a male voice exclaimed. "The idea, giving a prescription over the phone!"

Two days later my body shed itself of something that looked suspiciously like a piece of placenta. The doctor denied it. . . .

Back at home, my body began to recover. Since it was summer our schedule was more relaxed. We could sleep a little later, spend fewer evenings at meetings. Mark, now eight, kept me informed of what was going on in the backyard when the other two were playing there, leaving me free to get acquainted with the new baby. In turn, we let him go alone to friends' houses and to T-ball practice at a nearby park. Mark found T-ball a frustrating experience. He practiced diligently, but game after game, while his family (or at least one parent) looked on, he sat on the bench. The season was almost over; he was discouraged; but still he went to practice.

Standing at the kitchen sink one late August afternoon, I was aware of ambulance sirens wailing on the busy street a block away. Glancing at the clock, I realized Mark ought to be coming home from practice. The phone rang.

Did we have a son about seven or eight years old? A car had run a yellow light. Mark, hurrying home to ask permission to go swimming with a friend, had stepped off the curb the instant the light turned green. Lee flew out the door. Telling Tim and Becky to stay in the house, I quickly followed. They were gathering our broken son onto a stretcher by the time we reached the corner. Lee rode with him to the hospital. I went back home to the other children and waited for Lee's call. Oh, how blessed we were: a rib, a broken leg, bruises, but Mark was conscious and alert. As I waited for a sitter to arrive, I thought about the birth of this child. . . .

From the moment the Georgia nurse had awakened me from a drugged sleep to announce, "Miz Truman, you've got a great big baby boy!" we had loved him. Two weeks later when his life hung in the balance, God had sent doctors who understood pyloric stenosis and friends to help us financially. I could still see his tiny body weighted down with sandbags to keep him from moving after surgery, while his only nourishment moved through tubes. Such a difficult beginning. . . .

But within a week Mark was home again, with crutches and a cast clear up to his hip. And Lee left for youth camp.

I was furious! *Of course* he was the district youth director. *Of course* the camp had been scheduled before this happened. *Of course* he was supposed to be there. But it wasn't fair! A new baby, a son in a cast, and two other small children—and Lee was going off to youth camp for *a week!* I wouldn't even have the car! For seven days I stewed about the "church" always taking my husband away. If there weren't so many demands on him, he would have more time for his family. We—I—were certainly at the bottom of his totem pole of priorities!

Marriage wasn't supposed to *be* this way! But I lived through the week. . . .

## 8

By now the living-room carpet was hopeless. As the winter of our third year approached, four children, Sunday school classes, board meetings, and choir had blended the various traffic patterns into one gray blur. I felt terrible about it. In fact, I just felt terrible.

Lee had a new project going—this time, a sign for the corner. Since we were at the curve of the street, a main thoroughfare to the freeway, he was sure a four-by-eight-foot sign that could be read from both directions would extend the church's ministry with thought-provoking phrases. Once again the small cement mixer growled as blocks grew into a planter base, steel supports rose, and the face of the sign was put into place. When the words, SIN NOW, PAY LATER appeared, they slowed traffic and were quoted in the newspaper.

Neither of us had realized what a quantum leap a fourth child would be. Even with Mark in school, I didn't seem to have enough energy to keep up with everything. So when the opportunity came to spend a few days away we seized it eagerly. Home looked better the night we returned, and the kids were happy to be back in their own beds. Lee flopped down on the couch to read, and I went into the kitchen to fix some hot chocolate. With a pan of water in my hand I turned from the sink toward the stove, and there, leaping up the wall beside the hot-water heater, were flames.

I stood transfixed. Should I put it out?—or not? There was plenty of time to get the family—and probably most of our possessions—out of the house before the fire spread. The church would be rid of this "fire trap," and with the insurance money, they could build an educational building . . . buy a parsonage *away* from the church. Every minister's family after us would be grateful. . . . *Then* I threw the water on the fire . . . and learned a lesson about housekeeping. If one's clothes dryer sits in front of the hot-water heater, one had better keep the lint vacuumed out from behind the clothes dryer!

The longer we lived in this very public house, the more public it became. Lee's folks complained that the toys they gave the children were not being cared for. We explained that the only place the outdoor toys and tricycles could be stored was in the walkway behind the church, since there was no garage or storage building. On Sunday when the children came out of Sunday school, they headed straight for our kids' toys. Naturally they weren't holding up, with seventy-five kids using them every week.

And it was a rare day that saw fewer than ten people at the front or back door. They needed a key, or had a message to leave, or wanted to check on a meeting, or occasionally, someone just wanted to chat. Between visitors, the phone rang. On one particularly hectic day I counted the calls. From noon until bedtime, the total was *twenty-two!*—plus house, children, baby, meetings, meals, homework, doorbell, etc., etc., etc.

The week after Christmas, Lee's folks suggested we take a vacation in their trailer. We were delighted. Becky would have her fifth birthday in Mexico.

Now surely, somewhere in the world there is a family with four children that can go on a trip without incident. It didn't seem possible for us. When Tim tripped on an uneven sidewalk and knocked out his front teeth, I couldn't remember the word for either doctor or dentist from my five years of Spanish. (He couldn't catch himself because his tiny hands were stuffed in his pockets, holding on to precious peanuts!) But when the incident was over, we went right on traveling as if nothing had happened. They say children can adapt. What about *parents*?

Back home again, Lee plunged into preparations for a youth rally. Working with young people was a special joy to him, and this rally was expected to draw sixteen hundred. At least, that was the goal. The district youth council divided the responsibilities, and Lee's job was to bring the sherbet. After all, he had a station wagon. Have you ever *seen* enough sherbet to feed sixteen hundred teenagers? Do you remember the ambulance full of frozen chickens? By the time Lee got to the rally, so much frost had built up *inside* the windshield that he had to stick his head out the window to drive. Somebody wanted to know what kind of air-conditioning unit he had in that car!

But all I wanted to know was why I felt so lousy. Surely by now I should have bounced back from Nathan's birth. Maybe I shouldn't have had the fourth child. Maybe I just wasn't able to keep up with such a big family. . . .

## 9

"The tissue report doesn't look good. Frankly, I'm surprised. I didn't expect it in a woman so young." The voice on the phone belonged to the specialist whose office I had visited two days earlier. The walls behind his desk were covered with impressive documents, including one that pronounced him a member of the AMA Cancer Board of Los Angeles. "We'll have to operate—the sooner the better."

"Fine. Let's do it tomorrow."

"Tomorrow? I don't know if I can get a bed for you by tomorrow."

"Well, get me in just as soon as you can. I don't want to hear all the horror stories about the operations of every woman in the church."

Forty-eight hours later I checked into the surgery ward. Lee's mother had come (once again . . . ) to tend the children, and by going into the hospital before anyone knew, I truly had avoided all the stories. I knew they would only make me fearful. As it was, I thought I was ready—even for the answer to my first question when the doctor walked into my room the morning after surgery: "Was it malignant?"

"We won't know for sure until all the lab reports are back in three days," he began, "but it doesn't look good." He sighed. "We'll just have to wait and see."

It was 1962. I was 30. Nate was 10 months old. Tim was just about to be 4, Becky 5, and Mark 9. I wanted to see them grow up, take possession of their lives, marry. I wanted to travel, see some of the places Lee had talked about. And I wanted to write a book. The doctor turned his head away from my tears and said there *was* still a chance. Meantime, he was leaving the city but would be back on lab-report day.

So this was what the Crucifixion had been like? Cut down at thirty-three with unfulfilled dreams, disciples you'd worked with for only a few years—disciples who were only babes in understanding. Not even your Father or mother could go into death with you. Oh Lord, I'm sorry you had to die so young. And now maybe it's me. I've tried to believe. Help my unbelief.

Two days later, our booming-voiced treasurer came to see me. It was my first day without pain-killers, and as he talked the whole visiting hour away, I became more and more jittery. When he left I could not sleep. Dinner arrived, but I could only watch the clock. At seven, visitors would be allowed again. Suddenly the dam of fear and pain and apprehension broke. Tears flowed unchecked; I cried hysterically. A nurse rushed in to find out what was wrong—actually, she wanted me to be quiet. Loud crying in hospitals disturbs the other patients . . . and the nurses. A hurried call to the doctor on call produced a hypodermic, but instead of calming, I cried more loudly. They pulled the curtain around my bed, closed the door, and posted a No Visitors sign. I didn't want to see anybody—not my husband, not my mother who had just arrived from Michigan, not the church members. *Nobody!*

The room was almost dark when someone took my hand. Through my sobs I tried to focus my eyes. There knelt a man from the church whose name I didn't even know. Lee had conducted the funeral service for this man's mother several weeks before. "Wh-who are you?" I stammered, trying still to focus. He told me his name. *"Go away,"* I said. "I don't want to see you."

"Now Ruth, that's not like you," came the reply. "You know we love you."

"No you don't. You love *Lee*. Go away!"

It was all plain now. The man left, but I saw clearly for the first time in my adult life: *Lee* was the one who was doing all the important things. *He* was the one who pastored and cared for people. And *he* was the one who was loved and celebrated. All *I* did was change diapers and cook and wash dishes. And scrub rugs! No matter how hard I tried to share in his life, it was *his* life, not mine. And mine was about to end without anything accomplished. Not even my biological role would be fulfilled. I had given our children birth, but I would not be able to lead them into life.

Another hypodermic finally exhausted my tears and I slept. Tomorrow the doctor would return with the report.

Cards and flowers had begun to fill my room, and the next morning was no exception. Three more plants were delivered. The nurse said they were calling this room the flower garden.

I couldn't understand it. Why would anyone send me flowers, unless it was because I was married to Lee? I knew of no other reason. The morning mail arrived, bringing a new stack of cards. I had opened about half of them when my doctor breezed in.

"Well!" he exclaimed. "I've got good news for you. You're *one of the lucky ones!"* In a haze I heard an explanation about changing tissue that was not yet malignant. "I guess you'll get to see those kids grow up after all!" He checked my surgical dressings, flipped through the chart, tweeked my toe, and left.

"And on the third day . . . " My resurrection day. The sunshine streamed in the windows. Alive. Alive! *Alive!*

And the best part was that I knew now why I wanted to live! When I faced death, I had been shown life.

After a long time of rejoicing I turned back to the unopened cards. The handwriting on the envelope of one was unfamiliar, but the signature brought to mind one of the older women who lived alone. There were several such women in the congregation, and on Sunday morning when I stood at the door with Lee to greet the people, I tried to pick out something about each of them to compliment: a pin, a flower, the color of a dress. I knew they took special care to look nice on Sunday, yet there was no one to tell them they had succeeded. So I tried to do that.

I read the verse on the card and recognized it as one of those the women's society sold. Then my eye caught a tiny "over" written at the bottom. Turning to the back I read, "We missed your warm greeting on Sunday morning."

Tears flowed again—this time, quiet tears of happiness. Someone had noticed! It was something *I* had done, something Lee had no part in. And *it was important to someone!*

Finding a place to start living one's life is like finding a needle in the proverbial haystack. I found my place on the back of a greeting card. It wasn't a very big place, but it was a beginning.

## The End

To be continued . . .

1

If you're going to begin again, you might just as well do it whole hog (to borrow my grandmother's phrase). But nobody was more surprised than Lee and I when the D.S. walked past us on Thursday night during conference three months later and said casually, "Oh, by the way, Lee, you're moving"—and kept right on walking. Lee was stunned speechless. He didn't even ask where.

The congregation had the same reaction when Lee went home from conference on Sunday morning to tell them. He certainly didn't want such news delivered via the *Los Angeles Times*. I guess we should have been prepared for a move. After all, beginnings rarely occur without endings.

A week later Lee came back from a meeting with the new church's board. "I can't believe it, Ruth. I went with a list of twenty ideas, and I didn't present a one. They were ahead of me all the way!" Leaving our church may have been a surprise, but the new assignment seemed to auger surprises of another kind. "Oh, by the way," he continued, "they asked me if we needed help with moving, what with you only twelve weeks past surgery, so I said we'd take all the help we could get."

"What kind of help?" An alarm system was going off inside my head. "I don't want strangers rummaging through our household goods, hanging our clothes in closets, unpacking our old shoes and dusty china!" Knowing Lee, I was afraid that was exactly what he meant.

I was right. When we pulled up in front of the gray and white house on July 25, eight women were waiting. However, before we had known we were to move, plans had been made for Mark to visit my sister and her family in Hawaii, and as luck would have it, this was the very morning he was scheduled to leave. So now Lee deposited me on the porch, greeted the women already there, and left for the airport with Mark. I could get on a stage and sing a song or make a speech, but meeting strangers was still scary, even after three churches.

I shouldn't have worried. With admonitions for me to sit in the middle of the house and give orders, they began to unpack the boxes as they appeared from the van. There was laughter, good-natured teasing. Our dusty crystal was washed and put away, beds made, linens stashed.

Noon came, and so did lunch. We sat around the dining table, all slightly dusty and disheveled, and shared the meal. Lee had returned and left again for the church, where he was supervising the unloading of books and office materials. We had deposited the other kids with their grandparents, so we were able to work the rest of the day—but now with *friends,* not strangers. They had put us both completely at ease with their love.

The house was a welcome change. A modest lawn sloped gently up to a porch edged with roses, and three birch trees grew at one end of the lawn, directly in line with a window seat in the living room. In the back was more yard, a two-car *garage,* a *storage* shed, and a large screened building that once had been an aviary but now was a kind of picnic shelter. We promptly dubbed it "the bird house." Living space was a little short: a tiny eating alcove designed for four (not six), two bedrooms, and a den that had been the last pastor's study. (Oh well, Lee didn't like to work at home anyway.) But there were closets, cupboards, furniture! And the best part of all—the house was more than a mile from the church! We lived in a *neighborhood,* on a *quiet* street.

The church, too, sat on a hill. Tall eucalyptus trees graced the front of the property, and there was a *lot* of property. At one end stood a simple sanctuary—built, we would discover, by the people of the church over many weekends. In fact, an astute worshiper could see where the concrete between the building blocks had ended on one workday and begun on the next. Beside that building was a small wing which housed office, social hall, and church school "meeting places." Lee was to finish the construction, following the master plan. Finally!—the right person at the right place at the right time. Maybe the appointment system worked after all. . . .

The excitement of this new place eased the pain of letting go the old friends in our last church. Besides, in the weeks since my hospital experience, we had made some discoveries about ourselves. . . .

The doctor had sent me home from surgery with strict orders: no visitors or work for *six weeks!* I had argued that it wasn't possible. The church people wouldn't understand. And who would take care of the kids? Certainly my mother couldn't stay that long, and Lee's mother had already done more than her share. The doctor was adamant. We were to put a sign on the door telling people to go to the church office first. Lee was to try to be at the office so they wouldn't return to the house. And we would simply have to find a housekeeper. That was easy for the doctor to say; he didn't earn $4200 a year.

We put the note on the door and ran an ad for a housekeeper. Mother was vigilant. Nobody would get past her, she vowed. My second day home from the hospital, she had walked into the bedroom to see a woman standing on the foot of my bed, digging into the cupboard above the closet. "What are you doing?" she had asked emphatically. The woman explained that she was looking for Girl Scout materials that other ministers had always kept in that cupboard. "Well you can just get down from there and leave! Don't you realize that we've got a patient here just home from the hospital?" Mother gestured toward me.

"Well, I'll just be a minute," came the reply, as the woman continued her search.

"You won't even be a minute. You get down from there right

now. You've no business rummaging in their cupboards anyway." Mother showed the woman to the door.

My heart sank. It wouldn't work. No way! And the women who had answered the ad wanted more money than we could pay, or hours that scarcely helped. Mother rewrote the note by the doorbell. In large letters it said: NO VISITORS. Underneath in smaller print, people were directed to the church office next door.

By the end of the week I was hobbling around, gingerly holding the baby on my lap or reading to the other children. Mother was to go home in a few days, and still we had no housekeeper. That's when God sent Pat. She happened to be driving by when she saw the church sign with Lee's name on it. Not knowing our distress, she had knocked at the "no visitors" door. She definitely was not a visitor. She was an old and good friend from our mountain church who had recently moved to this city, but wasn't sure where our church was—until she saw the sign. Pat, who never had liked housework, would be our housekeeper. Dear, dear Pat.

And with uncommon common sense, she helped me to understand. My anger at the church for taking my husband, my distrust and frustration with critical church people, my lack of confidence in myself—these were all problems I had *let* happen. As a result of trying to please everybody, I had ended up feeling I was nobody. Somewhere in my new beginning, I had to discover myself, so I would be able to appreciate and understand others.

For six weeks, people did not knock at the door. They came and went next door, worked in the church kitchen overlooking the yard—even while I sunned on a chaise lounge—and did not call out. The telephone was quiet. And they showed me what I had not known: I could trust them. *They loved me by leaving me alone.*

So in the new church, when the youth who worked as the "pastor's assistant" sidled up to me on the first Sunday and told me I should sit in the "minister's wife's pew," I had new courage. "Where's that?" I asked. He indicated the second pew directly in front of the pulpit. "Oh, I don't think so," was my smiling reply. "I'll just sit back here," and his startled face as I took a seat two rows from the back was just the right beginning toward independence.

After church Lee told me to come see what he had found. Behind the sanctuary was a large headstone. "Can you believe it? Westminster may have Henry the Eighth, but *we* have Beatrice and My Girl, Polo Ponies Who Gave Their All at Midwick."

So we had moved from a church-by-the-wash to one that sat on ground once devoted to polo fields. It was very appropriate, for we both had come to understand that whether Lee was a minister or not, it was just his nature—to work like a horse!

## 2

There was more in Midwick's history than polo ponies. Once it had been a private country club with golf course, swimming pool, and tennis courts. Only a small piece of the original lands now remained—a city park, one corner of which edged the church property. The story goes that a Jewish gentleman had applied for admittance to the club and had been denied, so he simply bought it. He offered the facilities to the city, some of whose officers had been members of the club. They were outraged by his action, so they turned it down. He then took the next logical step: he subdivided it.

Into that subdivision had come young families with lots of children (the baby boom was booming!). A small congregation of Methodists had an inadequate building in a nearby older section of homes, and they had the good leadership and sense to buy the land on the hill. It was a tremendous venture for so few people. But as they began to build the sanctuary, some of the newer families came to help. By the time we arrived in 1962, it was a church just about to open into full blossom. Methodist ministers joke about being sent to two kinds of churches—challenges or opportunities. This church, eighteen minutes from the center of Los Angeles by freeway, was definitely an *opportunity*.

And Lee was ready. He wasn't *quite* so young now! Three churches (four if you count the New Jersey country church separately) had taught him a thing or two about being a minister that seminaries can never teach. He was approaching maturity in the Methodist tradition. He had experienced conversion (faith), gone to Bible school (Scripture), completed theological studies (reason), and served four churches (experience). And from his youthful occupation (and earthly father), he had learned construction.

The church members were ready, too. It soon required two services to fit the congregation in, and children were pushing out the walls of the small church school space.

Naturally there were a few changes. When the pastor's assistant we had inherited slipped wine into the Communion chalice because *he* thought that was the way it ought to be, regardless of Methodist tradition, Lee started looking around for other staffing solutions. A part-time youth minister took the assistant's place, and later a calling pastor was added. And more people came. . . .

In the first few months, Lee huddled with the building committee and trustees over the master plans. A few lines were redrawn to add more space at little extra cost, finances were gathered, loans secured. The fall and winter months of preparation flew past, slowed only by a December attack of flu. By March, groundbreaking day had arrived. Everyone literally dug in—church and city officials, children, Sunday school teachers. The teachers were especially excited, for they would finally have their own classrooms and space to store teaching materials.

Everybody hovered over the plans. Such a building this would be! The top floor, level with the existing buildings, would provide a large social hall with stage, kitchen, and restrooms. Downstairs at the parking level would be rows of classrooms opening to the outside, and someday a "Galilean" play yard was to be added, making possible a nursery school and/or Head Start program. It was a good thing excitement ran high that day; it would have to last for a whole year!

The winter at home was spent learning how to live in our new house. And were we living!—chicken pox, German measles, mumps—ten weeks, going around four children. As soon as one would go back to Sunday school, along would come another illness, and those that weren't caught at church were caught at school, where now both Mark and Becky were enrolled. But at least they were sick in *private!* For me that was a major blessing . . . and relief. Not only were there fewer people at the door, and those were usually neighbors, but the telephone also rang less. Lee's office was at the church and the people were used to calling there. Life was approaching something like normal.

The month before groundbreaking, Lee bought a Renault that had been abandoned by its owner in mid-street when it refused to go farther. It was so small that Lee had to put it on instead of getting into it, but it was all the family budget could afford. We had discovered that distance from the church had its disadvantage in transportation, but we did not realize that we had taken a life-changing step. Forever after, we would stay a two-car family.

The budget had to stretch again when a seventh family member was added—this time a purebred cocker spaniel given to our children. And the workload stretched, too, because she puddled whenever she was excited. With four kids, that was most of the time. . . .

But even with children, husband, congregation, and dog to care for, I found myself looking out the living-room window at the university that sat on the hill. It was a fifteen-minute walk from our front door. Long ago when I had taught school to put Lee through seminary, I said that if I ever went back to work in education, it would be as a counselor. Probably we'd never again live this close to a school where I could get a master's degree. But each time I began to think about it, somebody would get sick, or Lee would want me to entertain, and I'd put the thought away. Perhaps when Nathan was five and in school, I'd consider it again. Maybe it was a silly idea anyway. Mothers with four children just didn't go back to school in 1963, and those who dared to work were actually looked down on by other women. Besides, I was already thirty-two, too old for school.

And children take such constant vigilance. With so many children, it was easy to lose—or gain—one. For example, after church one day, Mark had piled into a car with the children of another family. They were all the way home before they realized there was an extra mixed with their five. But it was Nathan who really taught us about vigilance.

When we had finished greeting all the people one Sunday after church, I began to round up our four. After looking in every possible place, we could find only three. It was the independent two-and-a-half-year-old who was missing (shades of Tim's bike ride!). Finally certain Nate was not at the church, there was nothing to do but start searching the streets. Slowly, in two cars, with five pair of eyes on the lookout, we started toward home. Lee veered around extra blocks in the Renault. I took the regular route past the park, across the freeway entrance, under the overpass, across a major artery, past the schoolyard, and down the five long blocks of our street. Surely he couldn't have walked this far; we must have missed him. Or perhaps, like Mark, he had climbed into the wrong car. Someone would call. Finally, our automobiles merged at the corner and together, arrived home.

There stood Nathan on the lawn, grinning from ear to ear, and in his brand new words declared, "I came home all by myself!" Like a homing pigeon. We would soon learn that whenever he was bored, which was often, he headed for the parked car or, if close enough, home. Three years later when he started kindergarten, I never knew when he would walk in the door announcing, "It was boring there. I came home where I could do something int'rusting."

And *I* was the one who had to be vigilant. Lee dashed in and out, supervising the building, calling, counseling, preaching, administering. He became very good at praying on the run. Sometimes we laughed, remembering the words of the man in New Jersey—highest paid man by the hour. Lee was far below minimum wage by that scale.

As the fall of our second year approached, it seemed the construction would drag on forever. Lee felt tremendous responsibility, for even though the trustees were keeping a close watch on the workmanship, they could not be there all the time. By November, he was anxious to have the circular driveway finished before the rains began. It was with relief that he arrived one morning to see the headers going into place, but when he checked them with his tape measure that afternoon, he discovered they were only 3½ inches deep. The plans called for 4½ inches of asphalt, and Lee was determined that was exactly what we would have. A call to the contractor made it explicit that he expected new headers put in at the correct depth, and there were to be no excuses. All the asphalt required by the plans had better be poured.

The building increasingly occupied his mind and time, but never more than on the day the workmen returned to finish the drive. Pacing up and down the hill, he watched as the short headers were removed and the correct ones put in place. He was pleased to have caught this negligence, which might later have cost the church hundreds of dollars in repairs. He was at the lower end of the drive when Elsie, the church secretary, came running out of the office waving and calling. "Lee! Lee! You forgot the PTA. . . "

At a nearby school, three hundred people were waiting for Lee to speak. By the time he arrived, the audience was hostile, and the woman who had recommended "our new minister" was just plain angry. He had humiliated her personally. The contractor was supposed to build; Lee's job was to minister. Sobered, he struggled to rearrange his priorities. . . .

After all, I had rearranged mine. The university was just too much temptation, too close. Who knew how long we would live here? At least that's what Lee had said. "You'd better go now, Ruth. There will never be as good a chance again." So when friend Nancy offered to take care of Nathan while I went to classes, how could I resist? Besides, she had a foster child just a week older, and the two boys were best buddies. A year or two earlier I would have let the fear of gossip—what the church people might say—stop me. But not now; now I knew that life had to be *lived*. And with every A I brought home, my self-esteem rose. It was good to reclaim my intelligence amidst diapers and potty training.

On a beautiful March Sunday, the church rejoiced as the building was consecrated. Oh yes, along the way it had been lighted (remember Lee's formula?—lights, buildings, chimes) so that people could see the church on the hill night and day. And best of all, the building was full—full of children

143

learning about God, learning to pray, learning to love one another as Jesus had taught. And it was full, too, of their parents, who were forming deep friendships that would last a lifetime, along with Christian commitments designed for eternity. This was exciting ministry.

And still more people kept coming. . . .

3

The short vacation we had taken during the building project left us dreaming big as the next summer approached. Amsterdam. Paris. Venice. Rome. The magic of such words! Add an ocean liner out of Montreal, ten magical days at sea, another ship gliding across the Mediterranean into Alexandria, Beirut, Jerusalem. So what if you go subtourist class, stay in youth hostels, and have the responsibility for nineteen young people—and on the ocean liner share the task of overseeing *sixty-five* teenagers? Can you think of a better way to travel when you have no money?

All our youth and inexperience struck again. The church not only agreed to the venture, but helped raise funds for several of their young people to go along. They saw it as a life-changing experience, as did we. So during the spring, with the construction winding down, Lee and I, with good friends Fritz and Bert, plotted an independent (i.e, the conference *doesn't* pay their way) youth work team. They and another couple would take two groups to work in Germany; we and our group would go to Norway. Each month we met with our young people to learn about Norwegian customs and churches. Then just two months before time to leave, the word came: our work project was to be abandoned because of lack of funds for materials at the church in Norway.

Quickly, we shopped for another location. To our surprise, the government of Israel was responsive. They would like us to bring our Methodist youth to work and live with the Jewish people on a kibbutz. Would we like to come to Ramat Hashofet outside of Haifa? And by the way, was Reverend Truman a relative of Harry S.? A fourth cousin! Marvelous. The people of Israel respected President Truman above all others.

In late June, our whole family boarded a plane bound for Montreal via Detroit, with sixty-five Methodist young people and the two other adult couples. Mother and Dad met us at the airport in Michigan to load our four children into their car for a summer of small-town living with grandparents. And we were off. (In retrospect we really *were* off!)

Except for seasickness in an ocean storm that sent drinking tumblers rolling from one end of the dining table to the other and then back again (and team members to bed); except for a distraught captain's genuine alarm when some of our youths set off a string of fireworks over the fantail on the Fourth of July (a sister ship had burned at sea two months earlier); except for burgeoning shipboard romances (and the subsequent vigilance they required)—except for these things, the voyage was uneventful. Ten days of eating, sleeping, and playing. Ten days of deep bonding of team members and interteam friendships.

In Amsterdam, the new lovers bid tearful goodbyes as the teams split to go to their various worksites. Our group began the trek down through Europe, across the Mediterranean into Beirut. Quickly, we learned how to toss twenty-one suitcases through train windows, be *on time* for trains, sleep in the best available beds, go without showers, and eat simply. The rule "carry your own suitcase" became hard and fast, as typical tourist buying began to make them heavier—especially the one belonging to Wendy, who was collecting iron door-knockers. And all the while, we talked about Israel.

The four-hour stopover at the port of Alexandria gave us our first culture shock. Obviously we had stepped back into biblical times, as far as dress, poverty, and disease were concerned. On returning to the ship, we emphasized once again the importance of not drinking the water and of making sure that food was completely cooked. Our teenagers just nodded; we knew they were thinking that nothing could touch them.

Some of their jauntiness had disappeared by the time we climbed aboard our chartered bus in Beirut, an old open-window, school-bus variety. The weather was hot, and almost ten days of steady travel and strange food were beginning to take their toll. At least while we were on the bus, we wouldn't be walking quite so much. . . .

If you had stepped into the bus with us, you might have noticed first the sweatband around the driver's head and the crucifix hanging from his neck chain. Then your ears would have caught the five horns he was eager to demonstrate. Those items were most essential to our racing trip through the narrow streets of Beirut. With all five horns blowing, crucifix gripped firmly between his teeth, and sweat soaking the headband, our driver plowed his way through animals, people, and carts of merchandise. Everything in our path scattered for safety. Inside, we bounced completely off our seats each time a tire hit one of thousands of bumps and ruts. We knew this three-day trip would be no pleasure ride.

Out into the hot desert countryside we sped, stopping occasionally to see ruins, eat almost-cooked chicken at the "bus stop" restaurant, or try our luck at enclosed "pit" restrooms behind the Chevron station, with the local people peering around the corners to see our reaction. We were traveling ever farther into the past. Camels were mixed with horses, cars, and long-robed people on the roadway. But slowly we realized that though we might think we were going back in time, almost every man we saw was carrying two things: an automatic rifle and a transistor radio. It was a sobering thought.

The third day on the bus, we were all looking forward to our arrival in Jerusalem, a good night's sleep, and our crossover the next afternoon into Western civilization at the Mandelbaum Gate. Talk of these things was being bandied about when suddenly one of the boys yelled, *"Hit the floor!"* Instinctively we dived as a jet roared past just over our heads, its landing wheels missing the roof of the bus by not more than six inches. Back in our seats and bewildered, the situation was explained when a guard pulled us to a stop half a mile farther on. He soundly berated our driver in Arabic and, after much hand-waving and yelling, finally sent us on our way. Minutes later, we passed a stoplight alongside the highway. We had just driven across a military landing strip in the path of an oncoming jet, thanks to our driver, who thought he could beat the yellow light. How do you explain to parents that the team won't be coming home because their bus was hit by a jet? Israel was looking better all the time.

We had planned to spend the next morning sightseeing and shopping in Arab-controlled Jerusalem, then cross over to Israel through the uninhabited area known as no-man's-land. The sun had barely risen, however, when our new guide came pounding at our doors. "Get up, get up! The king is coming! You must go now. They are going to close the gate." Hastily we packed and boarded our bus.

"The king [Hussein] is coming to visit Jerusalem," the guide explained, "and to show our strength, our [Jordanian] soldiers have been shooting across the border. On the Jewish side they do not know what is happening, but they are returning the fire. It happens every time the king comes." All I could think of was Henny Penny, strutting around and shouting, "The sky is falling! The sky is falling!"

To protect themselves from the sun, Lee and the boys had bought souvenir Arab headdresses. In fact, they were all wearing them now as we entered no-man's-land. Our guide instructed our group to remain standing in the center of the area while he and Lee went to the checkpoint to clear our entrance into Israel. It was hot now, and the team was getting restless. Several cameras appeared and one fellow lifted his to take a picture (shades of Budapest!). The guide came flying back. "No, no, no!" He pointed upward. There above us at each corner of the open space were stacks of sandbags, and now we saw—from each one protruded the nose of a machine gun, pointed right at us. Shivers ran down my spine as a small mocking voice rang in my head, "Well, you *wanted* to travel, didn't you?"

Lee, meantime, was pulling his own faux pas. Somehow, in the time between our invitation to Israel and our arrival, his heritage had shifted somewhat—from President Truman's fourth cousin to his nephew. So it was that Lee's introduction to the guards at the checkpoint had initiated a flurry of phone calls. A public bus arrived and was put at our disposal. City officials appeared to greet us. Our guide, ever alert, saw their hurt, puzzled expressions as they stepped forward to shake hands with "Mr. Truman." A whispered sentence was all it took for Lee to hastily remove the offensive headdress and begin to apologize. How was he to know it was an exact copy of the kind worn by the Arab military?

In contrast to the bustle of Jerusalem and Haifa, Kibbutz Ramat Hashofet was a peaceful haven in the countryside, settled by people bearing the tattooed numbers of World War II concentration camps. They welcomed us profusely and we soon joined them in their work schedule: up at 5:00 and into the orchards or fields; breakfast break in the fields at 6:30; lunch at 11:30; and back to the fields until 3:00. The diet was always the same: hardboiled eggs, fresh vegetables, plain yogurt, the juice of whatever fruit was being harvested that could be added to mineral water for a flavored drink, and occasionally a small portion of chicken. Our boys were always asking for *two* eggs. They, especially, missed the protein of an American diet, and we were all losing weight.

Then it began. Was it the warm soda-pop, the uncooked chicken at Balbec, or just the change in diet? Whatever caused it, dysentery began to fell the team members. Valiantly they tried to keep working, relieving themselves in the weeds of the orchards (there was no other place when at work) and returning to pick their share of plums or sunflower seeds. In between, they enjoyed the good times, dancing and sharing with the kibbutz youth. Then, a week before we were to leave, Lee jumped off a loaded sunflower truck as it returned from the day's work, one foot slid on the gravel roadbed, and he lay suddenly motionless.

At the hospital in Haifa, as the paralysis from the back injury moved into both legs, the doctor told him he would probably never walk again.

"Impossible. I have to be on the ship next Thursday." The doctor ordered traction, which in that hospital meant hanging bags of bricks over the foot of a 6' bed and attaching them to the legs of a 6'2½" man who was supposed to lie flat. When the doctor left, Lee quickly discovered that no one else in the hospital spoke English. Not even *bedpan* or *water* got a response until they found a nine-year-old patient who could translate.

At the kibbutz, the care of the team was up to me now. We pulled together and vowed to complete our mission to the best of our ability. So when, as a thank you, the kibbutz arranged a picnic by the Sea of Galilee for their youths and ours, we all climbed into the field trucks for the jostling trip. The picnic would allow me to relax and forget responsibility for awhile. It was in the midst of a laughing moment that Vladimir, a Russian immigrant about thirty years old, scooted over next to me in the truckbed.

"I don't understand you," he began. "Here you have so much responsibility for the young people, you must handle the money, and your husband is in the hospital so ill. If you were a Jewish woman," he paused and put his hands over his face as if wailing, "you would be crying and mourning. It would be *so* bad." He rocked back and forth like a woman in distress. "But you are laughing. What is the difference?"

Suddenly I knew why I was in Israel, sitting in this truck. "Vladimir," I replied, "we are Christians. We believe—I believe—that Christ works everything together for good. The God of your father and mine will take care of everything."

Vladimir leaned back against the side of the truck, his arms crossed, his brow furrowed. "It is as I thought, then. It is your faith. We do not have that kind of faith." After several moments of silence he began to talk of other things, but we both knew we would never forget what had passed between us.

In the hospital, the doctors had suggested one last possibility, if Lee thought he could stand it. They would hang him by a leather sling around his neck, put the weight of a man on each leg, and with hypodermics, inject strong muscle relaxants. When the pain ceased, he must tell them; then they would wrap his body in a cast from shoulders to hips, immobilizing the spine in that position. Lee was desperate. He certainly didn't want us to board our ship in two days and leave him behind in Haifa, yet he knew I would have to leave with the team and travel at least as far as Paris, where our young

149

people could rejoin the other leaders and groups. He told the doctors to try.

How many times he passed out during the procedure, he never knew. He was only aware that he had been slapped on both sides of the face to bring him back to consciousness—again and again. And then finally the pain left and the cast went on. When we boarded the *S.S. Herzyl*, Lee was with us. God had indeed taken care of everything.

4

It must have been quite a sermon. Of course, neither Lee nor most other people thought it the least bit unusual. What *was* unusual was the envelope that was slipped beneath his study door that afternoon. The letter said that the woman had intended to leave $12,000 to the church in her will, but after listening to the sermon that morning she had felt moved to give it now. Lee was sure he hadn't asked for money.

As is often the case, there was a project waiting for funding. For several months after our return from Israel (would I ever want to travel again?), the trustees and parsonage committee had been considering whether to add on to the house. The conference standards called for four bedrooms and a study. We had two. Also, the city had condemned the birdhouse, so it had to come down. And our children were growing larger, while the kitchen eating area was shrinking proportinately.

I made a simple proposal: open a hall through the master-bedroom closet to a new large room that could either be divided into bedrooms with a movable wall, or used as a family room, according to the needs of the occupants. A trustee had a better idea. Drolly, he suggested we should put birth-control pills into the church budget! It was obviously too late for that, at least in our case, and since the money was now available to underwrite the cost, the design committee moved into action. They decided there should simply be two more bedrooms—and of course, a bath to go with them. That would match conference standards. But first we would look around to see if we could find a house already built that would be better.

Fifty houses later, we launched the renovation. While it was exciting, it was also kind of scary, since we knew we would have to live through the mess, and I was in my second year of counseling studies. With the decision made, I dropped one class and plunged in. The plans were drawn; the project grew. A door here, a porch there. The kitchen dinette wall would have to go. It would be a good time to replace some of the furniture that was worn out—and the carpet; so of course that meant new paint and paper. I had the feeling that this was turning into a whole lot more than my original simple room. But the frame for the new section was already springing up in the backyard.

Lee, meantime, was busy getting a nursery school and a Head Start program underway. The education commission had decided that both were needed, so the two worked out of adjacent rooms and shared the play yard. Our only question was which to enroll Nathan in. After all, our salary was low enough to qualify him for Head Start! The education committee solved the issue by enrolling him in the nursery school at half tuition. (It really didn't look right for the minister's son to be eligible for the government's poverty program. . . .)

Lee's sojourn in the hospital in Haifa and his medical experience in Africa had made him acutely aware of the true lack of medical equipment in so many places. Falling into conversation with a doctor at a Civitan lunch, the civic group to which he belonged in this town, he discovered that the plastic hypodermic syringes, which normally were thrown away, could be salvaged if they were properly cleaned and sterilized. So when the nursery school was running smoothly, he found some women to sort and clean the syringes that doctors all over town were willing to donate. Faithfully, the women sorted, cleaned, and prepared them for mailing to India. The unusable ones were thrown into a big barrel and put in the storeroom.

It was also time to add chimes to the church. But this time it would be a ready-made, commercial system. The speakers—for want of a steeple or bell tower—would be mounted on the highest point of the new building and would send their music across the housing tract. The installation was completed quickly, and the reaction was equally prompt. The woman across the street complained because they woke her up on Sunday morning. But it was the neighbor at the end of the building who made the most threatening objections. She would seek legal action if needed. Lee went to talk to her. Was it the angle of the speakers? The volume? No, it was the time. They were set to go off every day just as her favorite soap opera was ending, and she couldn't hear the TV. From that time on, the chimes played *after* the hour, during the commercials. On such small misunderstandings the work of the church is often broken. . . .

Meanwhile at home, holes were appearing everywhere. A new closet was being added to our bedroom, a door was cut to the new hall, the french doors in the living room were being removed, space for a dishwasher had been carved out of the kitchen cabinets. And the birdhouse was coming down. A good thing, too. When we returned from our summer trip, Tim had raced into the birdhouse in his joy to be home and explore every inch, only to come screaming out, his legs black with fleas! Water from the hose had knocked them off, but we could imagine that every board and crack was infested with eggs.

Amidst the confusion, I grabbed every available moment to study. My master's program had been approved, and I was now an official candidate—but it was a sixty-unit study, which meant two years full time, and I rarely could manage more than six units a semester. At that rate, I might as well quit. I would never finish. But Lee said, "No way." If it took five years, it didn't make any difference—the time would go by anyway. That was easy for *him* to say. The truth was that on some days, coffee was all that held me together. And Nancy. Her willingness to help tend Nathan never wavered. Without her, I wouldn't have been able to keep going.

By spring most of the heavy construction was over, so when Mark asked if he could have a slumber party for his twelfth birthday, I agreed—but just a *few* boys. Mothers of the world, take notice! Always give an exact number to such a request! *Seventeen* boys arrived, all between the ages of eleven and thirteen. The pillow fights, the street races, the skateboarding down the hill, the nonstop talk all night! When would I ever learn that my kids didn't do things in a small way? Mark was barely over a broken arm from skateboarding, and the only thing I could give thanks for that night was that he was the one boy not riding his skateboard.

The birthday party was followed by Easter—and such an Easter! By now the congregation had grown so that we needed five services to accommodate the Easter crowd. Lee started one; in the social hall a half hour later, Ron, our youth minister, started another. When the first service ended, Lee walked in to preach at the second, while Ron started the third; and Lee walked in to preach at the third while Ron started the fourth; and so on. They were all full, and Lee's exhilaration almost matched his weariness (huh?). He felt almost as good about Easter as he had about his private victory a few weeks earlier. . . .

He had struggled with the Renault for two years, so when the chance came to buy the MGA, he jumped at it. For someone who had raced cars in the concrete Los Angeles River bed, on the dry lakes, and on the ridge route, the MG held the magic of a true sports car. He had adjusted the timing and fine-tuned the engine until it purred. So when he saw the stock-car slalom advertised, he knew he had to enter. True, it was on Sunday, and there was an afternoon ice-cream social planned at the church, but the track was only twenty minutes away. If he timed it right, he could just sandwich it in between worship services and social. It was also a Communion Sunday, which meant he'd be wearing his clerical collar (shades of Rome!), but maybe he could pull his jumpsuit on over his good clothes to save time.

Determined that no one would know, he told me only that he wouldn't be home after church, since he "had something to take care of." He arrived at the track late for vehicles of his class, so he decided to run in the next class up. Pulling the MG into the starting line, he looked over to see a young and beautiful blond woman at the wheel of the adjacent car—a Corvette. There was no way he could beat a Corvette. Hot and perspiring, he unzipped the neck of his jumpsuit. The clerical collar underneath came into full view. The woman's mouth dropped open, the starting light went off, and Lee was gone before she recovered. As he loves to say, "It's in the books; an MG beat a Corvette. Only by a few yards, you understand, but it's in the books!"

It wasn't that he didn't have enough to do at the church. There were still two building projects on the plans, and he had begun to write a weekly column for the local newspaper. Even while the house was evolving, the decision was made to build the small music and choir building behind the sanctuary. This meant the storage room had to come down, and in it was the barrel of now almost five thousand bent and useless syringes. Lee wasn't quite sure what to do with them, so he called the police. "You can't bury them," came the answer, "and you sure can't put them in the trash. I'll be hanged if I know what to tell you. How many did you say you had? *Five thousand?* What church did you say this is?"

Several days later, the cement truck arrived to pour the slab for the music building. Suddenly Lee burst out of his office door. "Wait! Wait! Don't start yet!" The amazed cement workers watched as the Methodist minister began to dump hypodermic syringes onto the ground where the cement was to go. Lee just grinned as he emptied the last of them and indicated that they could pour the cement now. "The archaeologists will really have fun with this one," he commented as he went back to his work.

The other building project was the bell tower. It would stand close to the street on top of the rise, and high among its bells would be the carillon speakers. The design was beautiful. All it lacked was time and money. By now Lee was accustomed to receiving money from unusual places, but even he would chuckle all the next year as the tower began to take shape, knowing it was paid for by the contribution of a stamp collection—*Vatican* stamps!

Four full years were drawing to a close. We had learned so much! In fact, when we looked back, we were almost tempted to think we were finally getting the hang of the ministry—at least Methodist style.

Or maybe it was simply that we were maturing—getting "older." Certainly the pace wasn't any slower. If anything, it kept accelerating. In fact, the fifth year held great plans. I would graduate (finally!), Lee would build the bell tower, and Nathan would start kindergarten. And the house was almost finished. Becky was excited about moving into her new room, and Mark was looking forward to having his own room at last, after sharing with two brothers. After all, he *was* going into the eighth grade.

In addition, Lee and I both felt good about my new self. I had become open and trusting, really enjoying who I was for the first time in my adult life. When a fellow student had challenged me in an encounter group to "come out from behind that role of minister's wife and start being a real person," I had been devastated; but I had grown. And Lee was thriving, sure that his life was being invested wisely, that his decision to become an ordained minister of The Methodist Church had been a good one.

Meanwhile, the house construction had dragged on long enough. It was time to finish the painting. . . .

5

While I was bent double scraping old paint off the door frame, the telephone rang. Some day I'll learn not to answer it (but that hasn't happened yet!).

"Methodist parsonage. Ruth speaking"—fatal mistake number two; I should have said "Truman residence" and stopped there. The voice on the other end was that of a district superintendent—not from our district though, and, I assumed, not too threatening even though conference time was approaching. How wrong can you be? I handed the phone to Lee and went back to my scraping.

You can get a kink in your back from bending over too long, but from standing up too fast? "Move? They're crazy. They just don't know what's going on here! Look at this place . . . there's a hole in every wall in this house, and most of the plans are in my head, not on the blueprints." Maybe the man on the committee was right—birth-control pills should be in the benefits package.

"I promised him we'd go take a look, Ruth. We don't have to

say yes." Lee's reassuring words didn't reach my ears; they were closed while I was using my tear glands. Fortunately, three of the kids were at school and Nate at Nancy's. At least our trauma could be resolved without their eight cents' worth (that's 2¢ × 4). . . .

"Didn't you explain, Lee? Didn't you tell him that we are in a grand mess, that moving is just out of the question?"

"He's a friend, Ruth. We've got to at least go look." I took off my paint clothes, washed in turpentine, and put on my face and good clothes. Because of a fifteen-year-old vow to go wherever they sent us . . . (The New Testament instruction not to vow anything came creeping into my thoughts.) Oh, well, we'll just look. Things have changed—at least they're asking, not telling. That's an improvement!

Los Angeles was never my favorite place—at least not the heart of it. No trees, no mountains, no *green,* nothing to comfort my midwestern hangover. I thought of the birch trees outside our living room window, the kids playing on the lawn, brown shaggy dog at their heels. As we drove, we passed nothing but buinesses, office buildings, concrete.

A left turn, and the street began to wind upward until we turned into the parking lot of a beautiful church snuggled into the side of a green hill . . . just blocks away from the ugly concrete. I allowed myself to be delighted, amazed at the sudden change. The steep A-frame building was punctuated with glass—deepest blues, sunlit red, golden orange—inside, the colors flooded the quiet sanctuary. Natural wood and earth-tone carpets set a mood of peace for worship—a haven in the city. While Lee searched out the pastor, I tried on the church to see if it might fit my soul. This was a grand building; maybe a little too grand for us. Our commonness was surely obvious.

After a tour of the educational building and offices, we headed our MG into a circuitous route to find the parsonage. When the number on the curb matched the one on the paper in my hand, we sat speechless.

An immaculate lawn sloped gently upward toward a green-shuttered two-story white house that might have escaped from Georgia. Plantation colonials stood on the lots at either side. A young man with a tennis racket came running out of the house next door, stepped into an expensive sports car, and sped away. If we had walked clear to the back fence at the house where we now lived, we would just barely have arrived at the front door of this one.

"Are you sure we should go in? We're not dressed very well. . . ." I was suddenly aware of the faint odor of turpentine that still clung to me, and nobody sold the particular shade of green nail polish I appeared to be wearing. I really was a painted lady!

The doorbell chimed elegantly. The pastor's wife, forewarned by her husband, welcomed us . . . I think. I was busy coping with the polished railing of the staircase that curved into the second story. Perfect for a bride to descend—or more appropriately, a perfect railing for a kid to slide down while I was entertaining the women's circle!

Lovely cushioned couches hugged a massive fireplace in the living room, mahogany armchairs were pulled just right for conversation—intimate conversation by firelight, with soft music playing. The serenity of the lawn flowed into the room. One football would certainly undo that.

Atop the staircase were three bedrooms and bath, *Better Homes and Gardens* variety. Smaller than the ones we have, I thought. I envisioned them stuffed with toys and children—and all in line with the front door. Mercy!

Walking quickly through an outmoded kitchen (another one to do over!) we entered the "game room, or *family* room, if you have one. Do you?" Did we! If she only knew! The thought of our four children in this house was interrupted by the breath caught in my throat. I had never seen such a room. A pool table sat at one end, seemingly disconnected from the rest of the room, which looked out on a gardened backyard. Comfortable heavy furniture, overstuffed chairs, low tables, and yet the room expanded beyond them. Obviously, this was where one lived. The rest was just for show.

With a slight apology for the condition of the kitchen paint, our hostess brought us back into the formal dining room opposite the living room. She was about to explain that the furniture in this room was theirs and that we would need to bring our own, when the phone rang. As she disappeared into the kitchen, Lee and I stood close together, drinking in the elegance. My eyes touched the lustrous oak, the etched glass of the breakfront, the floral centerpiece.

Then I looked up. How could I have missed it? Hanging over all was a sparkling chandelier, the colors of its Venetian crystals dancing across the patterned walls, a crown jewel in a house meant to dazzle the beholder.

Transfixed, I began to giggle. Never had I seen anything so hilarious. So much laughter was rolling around inside that I could barely contain it.

"Ruth, what's the matter with you? What's so funny?" Lee whispered.

"The chandelier . . . " Our hostess returned. We bid a hasty goodbye, with Lee doing all the thank-yous. Talking was beyond me.

Halfway down the long walk, Lee demanded to know. What *was* I laughing at? What was wrong with the chandelier?

Tears were running down my cheeks. "Didn't you see it? Didn't you see that gorgeous chandelier? We can't take this church, Lee. We can't move here. Not us. Not *our* family. We have to stay right where we are. . . ."

"But what's moving got to do with the chandelier?"

Poor dear. All this time together, and he still didn't understand how God speaks—especially to me. Move? Us? Not on your life. For when I looked at that elegant sparkling chandelier, I saw. . . .

In a flash of insight, I knew . . .

In one week . . . there would be spaghetti—hanging—from the chandelier!

(P.S. We *didn't* move.)